When you realize there is nothing lacking,
the whole world belongs to you.
—Lao Tzu

YOUR SPACIOUS SELF

clear the clutter and discover who you are

SELF

STEPHANIE BENNETT VOGT

Hier**⊕**phant publishing

Cover design by Adrian Morgan
Cover art © istockphoto
Author photo by Daphne Weld Nichols
Text design by Jane Hagaman

Hierophant Publishing
8301 Broadway, Suite 219
San Antonio, TX 78209
888-800-4240
www.hierophantpublishing.com

If you are unable to order this book from your local
bookseller, you may order directly from the publisher.

Library of Congress Control Number: 2012944216

ISBN 978-0-9818771-8-1

10 9 8 7 6 5 4 3 2

Printed on acid-free paper in the United States

To Jay and Camilla.
I love you more than words can say.

CONTENTS

Part IV – Non-identification: Be the Observer

Part V – Compassion: Feel Good Now

Part VI – Wisdom: Reveal Thy True Self

PREFACE

We must be willing to get rid of the life we've planned,
so as to have the life that is waiting for us.
—Joseph Campbell

I was suffocating. Everywhere I looked there was *stuff* . . . and all that stuff was slowly squeezing me to death.

Then I came down with a garden-variety sore throat that I attributed to the stress of holiday season; this morphed into a fever, a cough that wouldn't quit, a bad case of insomnia, and my first-ever sinus infection, which was so painful that I thought I would go mad. The meds that helped relieve the pain in my head would deliver a terrible upset in my stomach. Placing my hand to contain one leak would uncover another. I felt like a ship that was running aground.

Desperate to fix this thing, I grasped at anything I could get my hands on: antibiotics, homeopathic remedies, teas and tinctures, vitamin pills. I ranted and thrashed and sweated. Nothing was working. I couldn't stand feeling so sick. I couldn't tolerate lying in bed like that, doing *nothing* but hacking my guts out. I couldn't bear not knowing what was happening to me.

My approach to any life challenge at that time had always followed a logical sequence: If something doesn't work, you fix it. You figure it out; you force or will it to change, if you have to. You *do* something about it. I had no concept that my body, in its infinite wisdom, knew exactly what it was doing to heal and rebalance itself. Bodies, like homes, are in a constant state of rebalancing all the time, creating and adjusting as they dance with the choices we make and the laws of nature. My job, if I had only chosen to listen, was to get out of the way!

A full-blown body rash seemed like a fitting end to a month of poor-me shenanigans. This last straw was so bad it was funny. And because I could finally laugh about it, I began to let go and (surprise, surprise) . . . to get well.

In hindsight, I can see how my body was simply reflecting the huge buildup of stress that I had not bothered to recognize for years. The stress was the cumulative impact of twenty years in the classroom, four years of invasive fertility treatments, and a major move from one neighborhood that had been home for nine years to a new home in a new town with a much longer commute. No doubt, my expanding collection of physical clutter was also a major contributing factor to this "perfect storm" I had created. I was forty-two years old at the time, a mother, a wife, a teacher, and I was burned out! I didn't know who I was anymore or what I loved. I had lost my rudder and all contact with my heart's longing. I had lost my way.

Sometimes we're so caught up in our heads that we need a major shakeup to get our attention. My healing crisis that winter showed me that I was seriously out of step with my true self. I knew that if I didn't address these early warning signs—like, *pronto*—things could get a lot worse.

So I did the unimaginable and gave notice. I walked away from teaching at one of Boston's preeminent schools. I was at the top of my game, and, just like that, I said goodbye to a twenty-year career, a senior position, a monthly paycheck with full benefits, and a community that had been family to me . . . to leap head first into the terrifying void of not knowing.

What was I thinking?

I wasn't. That's why I could do it.

Pulling the plug was no small achievement for someone so tightly wired to a daily routine, a professional identity, and financial security. All I could do for the first few months after quitting was grieve for the old parts of myself that I was deliberately dismantling—unaware that my little sore throat was like a pebble that had started an avalanche of clearing and transformation that continues to this day.

By releasing a huge part of my personal and professional identity, I was able to get in touch with the things that made my heart sing (and cringe): my passions, my longings, my fears—*my clutter!* For the superorganized neatnik that

I am, this last revelation came down like a sledgehammer on my self-concept and worldview.

As my husband once said, "Change happens slowly, then all at once." For months after I'd quit I simply followed my "knows" and improvised my life—sometimes making lame stabs at clearing out a drawer, sometimes doing things that made my heart sing, sometimes doing things that made no sense at all. There was no particular pattern or unifying principle or plan. I allowed my little "dinghy," now repaired and in much better shape, to float along looking for the next strong current.

Though modest in the beginning, the process of shedding my physical clutter seemed to grow organically and exponentially: Searching for a pen in a drawer that was jammed to the gills with every conceivable writing implement (including the pristine box of personalized pencils that I got when I was in grammar school) led to clearing that drawer and the one below it, which led to clearing the bookcase, then the piles of magazines with the mouth-watering recipes I never got around to trying.

Looking for a plastic food container led to recycling dozens of excess lidless yogurt cups, consolidating the condiments in the fridge, and tossing unidentifiable freezer items laden with inches of frost. Removing sticky bulletin board notices, dog-eared flyers, expired coupons, stale artistic masterpieces, and rubbery refrigerator magnets (selling pest management services) led to the long-overdue renovation project that opened up a dividing wall in our kitchen, added a fresh, colorful coat of paint, and offered a new lease on life.

The easy things led to clearing out more difficult ones, such as the clothes I might be able to fit in again someday (not), my daughter's adorable baby clothes, my matchbook collection, all my graduate school term papers, classroom notes, and twenty years of teaching paraphernalia.

Before I knew it, my clearing effort had grown into something way bigger than a string of random feel-good exercises. It became a journey—a journey that had much less to do with clearing out "things" than it did with clearing out my *attachments* to things.

Weeding out the material excesses of my home and life became an enlightening practice of *feeling* the experience of clearing. Feeling how congested or gummy or even nauseous I can be after an hour of moving junk around. Feeling how much my feet hurt or how clearing makes me more thirsty and sluggish. Feeling how hard and painful and embarrassing it is to let some things go. Feeling how good it feels in the house after I've put stuff in the recycling bin and walked it out to the curb for the Friday morning pickup. Feeling my feelings fully and completely without attaching any drama to them or taking them personally.

Turns out, I didn't need to go on a pilgrimage or meditate on a mountaintop to find myself. My home became my temple, my clutter was my teacher, and my journey of self-discovery began with clearing out a single drawer. If the purpose of life is to unlearn what has been learned and remember what has been forgotten, as the Sufi saying goes, I had inadvertently bumped into my curriculum. I began to remember what I had long forgotten: that I adore creating beautiful home spaces that feel good and nourish people. Even as a little kid, I was constantly building sanctuaries for myself, my dolls, my friends next door. I could transform a cardboard box into a palace.

Bundled together, the highlights that span the last two decades of my life could easily read like the catalog of study of a self-organized, nonlinear, graduate program. Intrigued by the larger questions of how our living spaces reflect us, affect us, and support us, I discovered and pursued a more intuitive branch of *feng shui* (a little-known field at the time) called space clearing. Training with some of the world's leading experts in the field led to two advanced-level certifications, the founding of a teaching and consulting practice, and a passion for writing (which I never expected in a million years).

Equally fascinated by the feminine principles—surrender, receptivity, self-care, mystery—that underlie my clearing message, I have devoted much time exploring women's spirituality, yoga, meditation, and energy healing, renewing the metaphysical studies in distance healing that I began when I was a teenager in Mexico City, where I was born and raised.

With all the study, life experience, and opportunity that I've had, I have to say that the most valuable takeaway from years in the clearing trenches is this: There is no replacing the wisdom that comes from living life in present time, embracing the shadow when it shows up, and entering each moment with innocent curiosity.

There is no crash course on how to evolve. You cannot buy clarity and wisdom at the store or manufacture it in a lab or train for it. Life does not always lend itself to being tidied or packaged, and our experiences do not always add up at the end of the day. No number of well-crafted summary points can capture the essence of a journey, especially when it comes to clearing our clutter. This is why it has taken me years to write this book.

If I had to summarize in three words the essence of the clearing path as I've experienced it, it would be these: raise, release, reveal.

I call them my "three Rs." Clearing *raises* awareness. Clearing *releases* attachments. Clearing *reveals* a spacious part in us that has been there all along. The three fit together as one organic whole. The more aware we become about the places we hold on, the more likely we are to let them go. The more we let go, the more spacious we feel. The more spacious we feel, the easier it is to clear the next thing or issue. Sound good?

If it were that simple, there would be no need for this book. You could stop right now and go "do" clearing. The thing is, clutter has no concept of simple. The clearing path is messy and meandering and full of unexpected surprises. Clearing clutter is not just something we do, like taking a class or going on a diet. It is a journey that is nearly impossible to measure, quantify, or even describe.

But I am a seasoned teacher, after all, and I love a good challenge. I love to extract the deeper truths from things and convey them in ways that people can understand and use every day. With nearly four decades of experience, I believe I have broken the code on this slippery subject. I'm ready to share what I've learned and offer a model for clearing that is both radical in its message and elegant in its simplicity; a model that comes field tested and uses *my* life as a principal source.

So here it is, from my home to yours: a book written by a teacher who is very much—and always will be—a student on the clearing path. A book that combines the ancient wisdom of space clearing with the modern practicality of clutter clearing in a way that everyone can relate to, use, and enjoy *every day.*

May this book reveal rich insights every time you read it. May it help you soften and release some of the colorful ways you hold on. May it guide, inspire, and support you to discover who you truly are.

ACKNOWLEDGMENTS

There is no way to explain what it is exactly that keeps people like us hunched over in a bad office chair for years on end, breathing life into something that we believe in so profoundly; massaging and molding a vision that doesn't reveal all of itself until the very last edit and redo; hanging in there when various body parts grow stiff, words don't come, and the "darlings" you loved madly end up dead in a heap on the cutting-room floor. It has to be the legions of visible and invisible helpers who are cosmically and magically aligned to keep us going.

So first and foremost, I would like to acknowledge Divine Intelligence and Presence, which is always on call and available to guide and witness. I include my own higher (spacious) self here. To this amazing aspect in all of us, that is way bigger than we even know, thank you for continually nudging us to keep evolving into the beings we were meant to be.

Thank you, Randy Davila, for believing in my vision, for inviting me to join the Hierophant family, and for encouraging a radical blending of two books that could reach (and help) so many more people.

To my editor, Eric Brandt, a heartfelt thank you for your gentle encouragement, brilliant insights, tough love, and unflagging willingness to roll up your sleeves with me and wade through and rearrange a massive amount of material. This was no simple upgrade, and I couldn't have done it without you. The same goes to the amazing editing and design team at Hierophant for making this book flow, show, and glow! Thank you all.

This book would not exist, either, without the previous incarnation of *Your Spacious Self.* Thank you to all who supported me in the early years to achieve liftoff for my self-published "baby": Nina Kimball, Meg Hirshberg, George Vogt, Ken Lizotte, Chris Banfield, Mary Lombard, Susan Page, and so many others. To all of you who purchased the earlier editions of my book and believed in my message from the beginning, thank you for your support! I hope you will agree that *Your Spacious Self* is even more energizing and "spacious"!

A deep appreciation to all the teachers who got me started on this path of awakening, who inspired me in my early years of space clearing, and who expanded the way I see the world. Though the list is way too long to include here, I'd like to add a special mention to Eric Dowsett, Desda Zuckerman, Karen Kingston, John Harvey Grey, Dr. Brugh Joy, Melissa Fountain, Katherine Woodward Thomas, Claire Zammit, Bambi Richmond, Janey McKim, and all my sisters at the Women's Well.

To all my readers, students, and clients who have joined me on this clearing adventure: Your stories of triumph and challenge, your supportive emails, your commitment and courage to *let go* inspire me every day. Thank you!

An appreciative shout out to my spirit sisters: Desda Zuckerman, for your gifts of healing and the amazing metaphysical romps we've had together over the years; Rose Thorne, for welcoming me into your magnificent Italian home and world as lady ambassador; Lisa MacDonnell, for your boundless support and friendship; and Nancy G. Shapiro, for your excitement and belief in this project and for holding my hand as I labored hard to bring her into being. Thank you all for enriching my life.

To my parents, Sharon and Jim Bennett, thank you for raising me in such beautiful home spaces and for letting me leave home at such an early age so that I could discover for myself what I was born to do.

To my brilliant and joyful redhead, Camilla-Bean, thank you for teaching me more about lightening up and letting go than any teacher by far. Seeing you blossom with so much self-awareness, humor, and grace makes being your mom such a privilege and a joy!

To Jay, my best friend and eternal sweetheart, thank you for being my steady rock—my shoreline—during my long dips in this vast (and sometimes choppy) sea of not knowing. Thank you, honey, for sharing this ride of a lifetime that stretches us both and keeps us laughing.

PART I

AWARENESS

TUNE IN

This being human is a guest house.
Every morning a new arrival.
A joy, a depression, a meanness,
some momentary awareness comes
as an unexpected visitor.
Welcome and entertain them all!
—Rumi

CLEARING WITH AWARENESS

The busy mind is so grateful to stop and taste eternity.
—Joan Borysenko

While I waited, bleary eyed and cranky, I proceeded to do what I always do while the coffee brews: I took the clean dishes out of the drainer, one at a time, and put them away.

On this particular morning, I experienced something I had never consciously observed before: In the sixty seconds that it took me to stack the last of the pots and pans, I noticed that the cobwebs in my head had cleared, and my mood was better. A lot better. The fog that I was carrying—and my spirits—had lifted.

What is this? I haven't even had my cup of coffee!

There it was: a spacious infusion resulting from a housekeeping ritual that I've repeated every day for most of my adult life; an experience realized and harnessed by simply being aware.

The truth is, I experience a swell of spaciousness *every time* I put the dishes away or hang the laundry up to dry or fold it. I feel the shift when I gather the empty cups and glasses in my living room or on my desk at the end of the day. Or when I address an annoying toleration, like replacing a light bulb or sewing a button or fixing the squeak in the door. I've devoted hours to writing about how simple actions can transform the energy in our living spaces, our lives, and our world.

I notice that every time I create an experience for my students to try at home or blog about ways to cultivate a clear home and spacious life, I myself am affected by the elegant simplicity of the practices I'm writing and teaching about.

What I didn't expect as I got deeper into my writing is that I would be responding to something more urgent: a distress call from people—women mostly—yearning to relieve the stress they feel; hungering to connect with something deeper and more meaningful.

Everywhere I go I see a longing for simplicity but a loss of *where to begin;* a desire for balance and nourishing self-care but no idea *how* to cultivate it. There is no time to juggle it all, let alone clear the things and thoughts that caused us to feel so overwhelmed in the first place! The chorus of unease that I'm hearing is a series of notes that sounds a lot like this:

◊ I'm overwhelmed. I have no time. I can't see straight or hear myself think.

◊ I'm so envious of people who are able to get things done.

◊ I have no idea what I love anymore.

◊ Slow down? You've got to be kidding.

◊ Where do I begin?

It's no surprise that our fast-paced lifestyles pack a wallop to the system. Technologies evolving at lightning speeds are making it possible for us to communicate as never before. We are assaulted by information all the time and have limited time to process even a fraction of it. Ironically, the very systems that are designed to simplify our lives seem to complicate them even more.

Add the noise swirling "out there" to the internal, chaotic struggles going on within, and you get fried circuits, a constant triggering of the fight or flight response, and a cascade of stress chemicals coursing through the system.

I wanted to write a book that cuts through the noise; one that could charm the part of the mind that is spinning out of control somewhere in "overwhelm La-la Land"; a book that creates the tiniest peephole of quiet, yummy spaciousness that not only expands with our awareness but can be felt—at the deepest level; a book that delivers a palpable experience of ease in one minute flat.

Your Spacious Self is that book.

Whether you are a superorganized neatnik, a hopeless clutterbug, a nonstop multitasker, a cautious beginner, an experienced professional, or a curious bystander—welcome! This book is for you.

IT'S A JUNGLE ... *IN HERE*

As you simplify your life,
the laws of the universe will be simpler.
—**Henry David Thoreau**

Here's what I'm wondering:

Are you wearing something right now that you don't love, doesn't flatter you, or doesn't fit perfectly (yes, including underwear)? Do you groan or cringe every time you walk into your home or office? Do you wake up in the morning worrying about something? Do you feel guilty when you take time to do something for yourself?

That was just the warm up. Here's what I *really* want to know: Did any of these questions elicit a physical sensation of any kind? An eyebrow raise? Constricted breathing? A gulp or a nervous laugh? An impulse to cringe, manage the situation, or bolt?

Were you aware of a change in your energy level? Were you aware of how the room feels? Were you aware of yourself being aware?

Welcome to my world of clearing!

IT'S NOT ABOUT THE STRESS OR THE STUFF

No one would argue that most of us do too much or have more possessions than we need. Or both. With our lives swept up in a swirl of attachments, worry, and endless, mechanical "doing," our minds become fuzzy on what stays and what goes, what matters and what doesn't. As humans, it is in our nature to experience clarity and spaciousness all the time. The problem is that we lose focus, get off balance, and forget how.

So how do we dial it back or even begin to reduce the noise, release the stuff that doesn't serve and support us, and connect with that which makes our hearts sing?

One minute at a time. In present time.

No matter how minuscule the task or effort, the fact is that clearing anything consciously and gently, as this book teaches, creates an energetic opening—a spaciousness—that will work on you slowly and surely to soften your attachments to things, beliefs, and outcomes.

Whether your clutter challenge is the stuff spilling out of the closet or the noise spinning around in your head, or both, here's what I know for sure—distilled to its bare essence:

◊ Clutter (and chatter) is not the problem.

◊ We do not need fixing.

◊ Without awareness, there is no clearing.

Let me explain.

In the end, it is *not* about tackling the unsightly messes, the boxes of who-knows-what mildewing in the basement, or the clothes that don't fit.

It's not about the mountain of mail, the emails that invade your inbox, or the pile of medical bills that the insurance company refuses to cover.

It's not about the car that needs new tires, the crazy-ass housemate who won't turn her music down, or the neighborhood dog that barks all night.

Nor is it about "fixing" yourself.

It's not about the despair you feel over the dishes that no one bothers to wash and put away, the to-do lists that get longer by the second, or the fact that you have zero time for yourself.

It's not about the hopelessness you feel, your inability to say no, or the fear of someone discovering your dark secret.

Clearing is not about any of those things. It is how . . . you . . . *relate* . . . to . . . them.

It is the space *between* the problem and the solution where the real juice is, where the real clearing happens. And the only way to release what isn't working for you is to enter that sometimes-scary zone called *feeling*.

Feeling the overwhelm, resistance, attachment, guilt, sadness, worry, despair, shame . . .

Feeling it all—without judging it as good or bad or taking it personally.

IT'S NOT ABOUT FIXING

We do not need fixing. The core of our being is not broken. We humans are simply out of touch with our true selves and out of balance. And, by extension, our homes and world are out of balance because *we* are. Not the other way around.

When you can allow feelings to arise in all their messy glory without fixing or judging or personalizing, that is when the clutter you experience "out there"—in your home and life—magically melts away.

No matter what your clutter challenge is, as you practice clearing in this way, you'll begin to notice some shifts taking place in your life. Who knows what that might look like for you. It might start as a tiny peephole of space that wasn't there before. An *ah-ha*. A kindness. A quieter dog. A surprise check in the mail. Less junk mail. Fewer pounds. A job offer. Fewer buttons getting pressed. Better sleep. More energy. More joy.

More you.

More real, spacious you.

CLEARING IS A JOURNEY

To the degree that you can see clearing as an adventure—a Hero's Journey, of sorts, that will take you places within yourself that you've never experienced before—here are some ways to gain the most from your experience.

INSERT AWARENESS

As you probably already know, or will soon discover, clearing anything has a sneaky habit of pressing our buttons and bringing up what I affectionately call the "weather." Many of the lessons in this book are intended to gently produce this emotional weather—on purpose—so that you can directly experience what your holding patterns look like. The Clearing Practices and the open-ended statements in the Clearing Journals are designed specifically to pinpoint and "needle" areas of stuckness, limiting beliefs, and resisting patterns in your life so that you can name them, feel them, and *let them go*—for good.

SLOW DOWN AND SIMPLIFY

If you are a take-charge, "doing" machine, the practices in this book might take a little getting used to. Don't be fooled by their simplicity. If the slow-drip model offered in this book feels grossly inadequate next to your Mount Everest of stress and stuff, take heart. Literally. The heart knows. The chattering, grasping mind—what the Buddhists call the "monkey mind"—is not equipped to deal at the level that is required.

It will help a lot to set clear boundaries: Limit the time you spend on each lesson and practice; stop immediately and exercise self-care whenever you feel tired and hungry. Drink a lot of water, as clearing is very dehydrating. Set a timer if you need help managing your time and energy level. Most of all, keep it simple and follow your "knows."

REFLECT AND RELEASE

Writing down your experiences (dreams, synchronicities, *ah-has*) is one of the most powerful ways I know to acknowledge and mark the shifts that are occurring in your life as you clear, especially when it feels at first like not much is changing.

As one of my students shared: "I have a hard time having my journal by my side, taking myself seriously enough to do the lessons. Today something clicked. I wrote and wrote. All the questions leading to one answer—*It's a way out!*"

Start your journey with a brand-new journal, notebook, or blank book. Use it to complete the daily contemplations, set intentions, integrate key principles, explore questions, gather your thoughts, and brainstorm ideas.

Best of all, when you use it especially at the end of each chapter (or day) to download, vent, wonder, noodle, integrate, reflect upon, off-gas—anything that is going on for you—you will be releasing loads of mental and emotional clutter!

SUPPORT THE JOURNEY

In this journey, there are two things you can almost count on: First, there is no way to predict what will happen as you clear; and second, no matter how good your intentions may be, if there is a monkey mind lurking in your head space, it is easy to fall off the wagon, get discouraged—or plain lost.

For that reason I am including these reminders to help bring you back. Write them down in your journal or on a Post-it note. If you can remember to adopt these guiding principles as part of your daily practice, I can almost guarantee that you will clear more stress and clutter than you ever imagined possible.

- ◊ **Be Curious.** Enter your life with wonder and curiosity. Pretend that you know nothing. Be willing to be pleasantly surprised.

- ◊ **Allow Silence.** Silence creates openings and opportunities to feel. Don't be afraid of it.

- ◊ **Invite Mystery.** There is no way to predict what will happen. Accept mystery in your life as a legitimate state of being.

- ◊ **Take Your Time.** Clearing is a journey to be lived, not a task to be completed by a certain deadline. Go as slowly as you need to, but keep moving. When you are rushed, vital connections are lost.

- ◊ **Stop and Feel.** The daily practices will open you up to new information. Notice and allow emotional weather to arise without taking it personally.

- ◊ **Don't Identify.** Most of what you'll be feeling is stuckness that comes from the past, from other people, and from your (and other people's) living spaces. The weather will always pass to the degree that you don't make it "yours."

◊ **Have Fun.** Don't take yourself or anything that happens too seriously. Being less attached to an outcome will make it easier to clear; it will raise your energy level, expand your perspective, and lighten your load.

WHAT IS CLUTTER, EXACTLY? 3

As long as a man stands in his own way,
everything seems to be in his way.
—Ralph Waldo Emerson

It starts with an eye roll and a nervous laugh that suggests, *You don't even want to know what I have lurking in my basement.*

This is the usual reaction I get when people ask me what I write and teach about. Some even get so nervous that you'd think I was going to send in a SWAT team to bust them on the spot for *even having stuff.*

Conversely, if my response elicits a glazed or bored look, I can pretty much guess that this is a person who cannot relate to clutter, either because she doesn't suffer from physical excess at all or is too busy to notice that she has any.

If, however, the mention of clutter is met with prickly resistance, a wave of emotional charge, a hollow stare that points to deep pain and shame, then I'm really interested. This is the kind of "clutter" that gets my attention—*and* all my "special forces teams" bearing massive and gentle amounts of love and compassion.

No matter what your housekeeping habits and lifestyle predilections might happen to be, if you live in a body that gets out of balance, thinks thousands of thoughts a day, feels pain and loss and fear from time to time, or gets caught up in worries of the moment, *you've got clutter.*

MANY FACES OF CLUTTER

As you can see from the sample of comments below, clutter shows up in many forms. It usually shows up in overlays of physical stuff, mental chatter, and emotional charge. Can you guess which is which?

> "I have tried so many ways to clear my home—life coach, junk removal, nifty closet systems, sweat and tears, and I usually end up again in a frozen state of clutter and disorganization. My moods are horrible when dealing with *my* stuff. I get angry at everyone, although I know deep down it is not their fault."

> "I struggle with busyness . . . always somebody wanting something: time, energy, money, etc. And I nearly always accommodate the request, wanting to be the 'good girl' and wanting to be liked. . . . However, I always end up feeling like there is nothing left for me—time, energy, or money."

> "I have lifetimes of projects. Why do I have so much material for so many possible projects that never get finished?"

> "My self-sabotaging brain is relentless."

> "I have been feeling irritable, anxious—just not right, not myself. It has been very difficult and painful."

> "I haven't had anyone over to the house in years. I am so ashamed of how bad things have gotten."

> "I feel overwhelmed . . . [embarrassed, sad, unrealized, guilty, trapped, weighted down, scattered, strangled, stuck, blocked, distracted, paralyzed, anxious, like a failure, hopeless, exposed, vulnerable . . .]"

Can you see yourself in any of these? Do any elicit even the tiniest flinch of self-awareness?

If so, you have just discovered the secret doorway to living clear.

CLUTTER REDEFINED

Clutter, first of all, refers to *anything* that gets in the way of experiencing your most spacious self. It is visible and invisible; it is any thing or thought that makes you feel off center and rattles your cage; it is the limiting beliefs that cloud who you are; it is stuck energy.

My definition is much broader than usual and includes myriad ways that we humans hold on and create imbalance in our lives. I'm sure you have one or two issues kicking around somewhere; if not in your home, most likely they lurk somewhere in your life.

Second, there's being clutter free, and there's being spacious. As you will discover, these are not always synonymous.

Clutter is a relative term. For some people, a wildly messy home or workplace can be nourishing. For others it can be annoying or downright disturbing. Your home may be beautiful and have perfectly appointed everything and still be "cluttered." Why? If you (or previous occupants) have experienced stress, internal pain, suppressed emotions, or cannot embrace the issues that are plaguing you, you create a different, energetic type of clutter which can be just as harmful—or even toxic—to yourself, your home, and the environment at large. This invisible form of clutter shows up in all manner of ways and could fill another whole book. For our purposes, I will simply refer to Mental Clutter and Emotional Clutter.

If you're still not sure you have clutter in your home or life, you can try this little acid test:

◊   I am living my best life.

◊   I am doing what I love.

◊   I can get through the day easily without a fear thought or one of my buttons getting pressed.

◊   I accept things as they are.

If any of the phrases above elicited a "no" response, there is probably a little (visible or invisible) clutter getting in the way.

CLUTTER TALKING

Though I try my best not to make any promises, it is fair to say that you will discover your most spacious self if you're first willing to *feel* the feelings that come up when you clear. Our body, with its five primary senses, is one of the most powerful resources we have for giving us feedback, should we choose to pay attention to it.

At the same time, I can predict that you will also bump up against your most contracted self as you clear. You'll recognize this when you feel yourself getting cranky, tired, spacey; you'll want to avoid, overeat, or hold on even more. You'll recognize this "small self" when you hear your inner critic find every reason to discredit your efforts, convince you that this clearing thing doesn't work for beans, and that this book is probably the worst one you ever read. If any litany of judgments derails you, remember: *This is the "clutter part" of your mind talking, not the real you!* The first step is to try not to give in to all that noise.

Another one of the points with which the small self might take issue is the notion that the practice tools are just "way too easy." It is amazing how much our little monkey minds like to complicate our lives. When offered a way that is extraordinarily simple, we balk. Hand us the keys to the kingdom, and we think there's got to be a catch. It can't possibly be this easy! Again, memo to self: *clutter talking.*

Our cluttered minds have zero concept of simple.

CLUTTER IS A STATE OF MIND; CLEARING IS A WAY OF BEING

Spaciousness?! You've got to be kidding. I can't even get past the piles of paper and the junk in my basement! If this (or some version) is going through your mind right now as I go into my song-and-dance spiel about the bigger picture, it might help to know that you are not alone.

Do any of these thoughts ring true for you?

◊ **Overwhelmed:** No matter how hard I try, I just can't seem to manage the sheer volume of stuff.

◊ **Been There, Done That:** I've bought the books on clutter clearing; I've smudged my entire house with sage; I've practiced some of the suggestions on simplifying that I read in

Real Simple; I watch HGTV religiously. Nothing I do makes any difference.

◊ **It's Not Me:** It's easy for me to get rid of stuff, it's my husband [wife, mom, child . . .] who has a hard time letting go of things or who *doesn't even see* the piles.

◊ **Spent:** I've spent gobs of money on closet systems, containers and baskets, professional organizers, even therapy . . . but my clutter remains a source of pain, shame, and embarrassment.

◊ **Two-Sided:** My office desk is perfect. My desk at home is a disaster.

◊ **Controlled:** I am a neatnik. I control my chaos with order.

◊ **In Denial:** Clutter? *Me?* I hold on to nothing. I get rid of things as soon as they come in the door.

◊ **Fearful:** What will become of me if I let this thing [thought, relationship, resistance, worry, status symbol] go?

◊ **Attached:** My stuff needs me.

Despite the proliferation and popularity of how-to books, makeover reality TV shows, *feng shui* cures, online support one click away, nifty containers and closet organizing services that are worth billions of dollars a year, and a self-storage industry bigger than McDonald's, Burger King, and Wendy's combined, clutter continues to grow; it is quickly becoming one of the biggest epidemics of our time.

Underlying the dizzying facts is the unrelenting message that if we simply banish this curse, we will finally find true heaven on earth. The standard view sees clutter as a "thing" that is separate from us; a nuisance or growth that we must extract, conquer, outwit, or reorganize back into orderly piles. And, like a strict diet that that must be endured, clearing is considered about as compelling as a root canal.

So what gives? With all the attention given to the problem, why is it that most clearing efforts, though well intentioned, do not last? Why do our homes and lives continue to be so stressed, stuck, and out of balance?

Most traditional approaches do not consider the energetic impact of clearing: that clearing one small thing or issue with intention, every day, is more powerful and sustainable than binge-clearing a whole lot all at once. We are more likely to throw in the towel just when things are beginning to shift, quietly, under the radar of any discernible progress. We might lose faith precisely when we should *not* be giving up and giving in to the agitations of the ego—the part of us that is only concerned with our comfort and keeping things the way they are.

Another reason why many methods of clearing and organizing do not work is that they promote an active and linear process of clearing, like a problem to be fixed, managed, or solved. In our Western culture where action reigns supreme, if we can't *do* something or make something happen *now,* then we are wasting our precious time. Going slowly and waiting to see what happens is a hard sell for those looking for immediate results. These linear approaches completely dismiss, and miss, the equally powerful receptive elements of clearing that invite us to slow down, allow, listen, surrender, feel, soften, *let go.*

Most clearing efforts do not make room for us to feel our feelings, honor our ebbs and flows, create a container of safety, embrace our shadow side, or allow us to be more compassionate with ourselves. The *modus operandi* focuses on the end result, not the journey; on our intellect, not our innate wisdom; on throwing away, not letting go.

Until we begin to make a shift in our mindset that recognizes and embraces and includes the feminine aspects of clearing, we will not begin to change our lives nor bring change to the planet. It is, in fact, this more balanced treatment that takes us beyond clutter freedom into the vaster territory of our most spacious self.

Radical in its simplicity, this paradigm shift in clutter clearing is really good news for everyone, including those who believe that they don't have any clutter at all!

PHYSICAL CLUTTER

4

It's terribly amusing how many different climates
of feeling one can go through in a day.
—Anne Morrow Lindbergh

GOING TO GOODWILL

In the past two decades of clearing clutter, I have had bouts of feeling totally lost and longing for those comfortable parts of myself that I have released, even though I know in my heart that they no longer serve me. My clearing anxiety has been so great at times that I have found myself on the verge of asking for some of my things back—from friends, from the consignment clerk, from the Goodwill attendant.

I have driven away from a consignment store completely bereft, analyzing to exhaustion the myriad scenarios under which I could have made good use of the object or outfit I have just given away.

I know it was too small, but was it?

My inner state of mind is such that you'd think I was Sophie from the movie *Sophie's Choice,* giving up one of her kids to the Nazis. This anxious diatribe lasts anywhere from fifteen minutes to twenty-four hours. After that, I find that the "fever" usually breaks, and I can get on with my life without as much as a backward glance.

Not all of us are like this (or this bad), of course. But I would wager that most of us have a very special brand of holding on.

What is your thing? What might your special "grip drama" look or feel like to you? Under what circumstances do you notice yourself holding on so tightly that you get rope burn? In what ways do you block and resist the whole being that you are?

Here's how one of my holding patterns has played out more times than I'd care to admit. I call it the "death march" to the Goodwill truck, a drop-off trailer that is permanently installed in the back corner of our supermarket parking lot. The scene is this: I stuff the trunk of my car with huge garbage bags full of clothes and shoes, handbags, kitchenware, old sheets and towels, then drive them two blocks to the trailer with a mix of eager determination, relief, and dread. I force myself to chant my mantra: *Ahh, this is going to be great . . . I can do this . . . no big deal . . . it's easy . . . see . . .*

I feel tension beginning to build inside me.

As I pull my car up to the truck I am rocked by the familiar jolt: *Ohmygod, I can't give away the beautiful green hoodie jacket my baby girl wore for three years. I can see her running and laughing in that thing with her curls bobbing out of the hood. It's in such perfect condition. And those cute baby shoes! Maybe I could make some kind of art mobile out of them and hang them in my house somewhere. I've seen people hang them on their rearview mirrors or coat them in bronze . . .*

Yet again, my monkey mind has completely taken over.

I could use those sheets for . . . well . . . I don't know what . . . oh yeah, the mummy costume we talked about. I know they'll come in handy one of these days (as they sit in the basement mildewing). *And the earrings I got from my grandmother* (and never wore) . . .

And so it goes . . .

I don't think I can do this!

I force myself out of the car and make my way to the trunk, palms sweating. *Breathe, Stephanie, keep breathing . . .*

I search for that jacket in the bag and pull it out. *I can't give this up. She was so cute in it.* (Holding up to my nose) *Oh, and it still has her smell, her joy, her energy . . . I can't give away that smell!* I tuck the jacket way into the back of the trunk where the attendant won't see it.

I hand the rest of the bags over to the attendant. I feel unsteady, nauseous. My wavering resolve is becoming a big heap of mush on the pavement. I grieve. *I hate this, I can't stand this feeling! I feel so sad, so empty, so . . . uh . . . wait a minute . . .*

Then it happens.

It's an itty-bitty wee awareness that nudges itself through the ego-mind's fear lock. Almost imperceptible . . . *Yes, is it possible? Do I feel even a teensy bit lighter? Can it be that I'm able to breathe just a little easier?*

I take in my first deep breath since I came home. *It's okay. I survived. I made it.* It almost feels good.

Later I think, *What the heck was all that drama about!* My daughter's jacket goes right back into the give-away box for the next time I take a carload over to Goodwill. I think I finally did let that one go—after about five tries.

CLUTTER AS WEATHER

Many Goodwill adventures later, I am slowly but surely learning to separate the noisy dramatics and heart palpitations from the more peaceful, go-with-the-flow acceptance. I now see these dramas as holding patterns that are part of a larger "weather system" that is unique to me. I've become so aware of the passing nature of these patterns—like clouds moving in and out or squalls intensifying and easing—that I now reframe any event, emotion, or physical sensation that does not reflect my most even-minded, spacious self: It's simply *weather.*

Sweaty palms—weather. Shallow breathing—weather. Worry that I made a mistake—weather. Worry that they don't make outfits like the one I just gave away—weather. Worry that someone will not care for my old laptop as well as I have—weather. Worry that I'll never find another one like it—weather. Memory of having something taken away from me as a child—weather. Grieving loss—weather. Tears—weather. Fear for the future—weather . . .

Contrast those patterns with: acceptance—*not* weather. Trust that there is more where that came from—not weather. Spacious detachment—not weather. Witnessing the weather—not weather. Pure, clear, and uncluttered, these states of being are the real deal.

PHYSICAL CLUTTER DEFINED

Physical clutter is the most familiar member of the clutter family, because it is visible and identifiable; it is the stuff we see, bump into, and wade through every day. If you can answer yes to any of the statements below, then you have some physical clutter:

◊ I have things that I longer need, use, or love.

◊ I have things that no longer fit me.

◊ I have things (projects) that are broken, not maintained, unfinished.

◊ I have things that do not have a dedicated "home" and/or do not get put away.

From an energetic standpoint, physical clutter is the grossest, densest form of holding on. Because of its high visibility factor, the good news is that it can show you the way out!

CLEARING PRACTICE

The first step in clearing clutter is to recognize the many ways clutter plays games with our energy level and our mind. It is always important to remember that these weather patterns are not who we are, and they actually do pass if we choose not to identify with them.

TUNING IN TO PHYSICAL CLUTTER

Below is a list of ways that clutter shows up physically in our lives. I invite you to cover the exercise with a card or piece of paper and slowly move it down to reveal one line at a time. Notice how you feel after each item. At the end of the list, take a moment to stop, close your eyes, and notice how you feel in general.

Notice if any of these patterns press your buttons, elicit sensations in your body, and/or trigger a memory, image, thought, or emotion. Once you've identified a feeling or a pattern, allow it. Don't try to analyze or fix anything. Just notice it. Feel it.

A word to the wise: Believe it or not, this and the subsequent practices that appear in this book have powerful energetic signatures. Words that are written down have as much power as spoken ones. They can elicit strong physical and emotional reactions when you hold a charge around them. The purpose of this exercise is to become more aware of the places you hold on by simply observing (by feeling) any charge as a data point. If you find yourself feeling jangled, overwhelmed, distracted, tired, or even ill, stop the exercise and take a break. Drink a glass of water. Get some fresh air. Repeat to yourself, "It's not mine." If you don't feel a thing, that's fine, too. In the world of sensing, there is never a right or wrong answer—ever.

◊ piles, stacks, towers, papers . . .

◊ unread articles, books, magazines, newspaper clippings . . .

◊ jammed closets (drawers, cubbies, corners) . . .

◊ dust, cobwebs, dirt, grime, filth, mess, mold, mildew . . .

◊ out of order, lost, broken, scratched, dismembered, mismatched, misplaced, disorganized . . .

◊ missing, stuffed, confused, scattered, spilled, stuck, chaotic, noisy . . .

◊ stink, foul, putrid, dark, cloudy, scummy, dank . . .

Stop and feel: Once you've had a chance to go through the list, close your eyes for a second. Notice any thoughts, feelings, and/or new weather showing up for you right now. Notice your breathing. Remember: There is nothing to do but observe, allow, and experience these patterns as symptoms of imbalance.

CLEARING JOURNAL

Take a moment to reflect in your journal how clutter shows up physically in your life.

◊ What stood out for me after doing the scrolling exercise was

———

◊ Some of the ways that physical clutter shows up in my life are

———

◊ When I tune in to the physical clutter in my home [other people's homes], I *feel* _____

◊ One thing I can do right now [today] that would make me feel better is _____

MENTAL CLUTTER 5

Mind is the projector, and the world is the projected. Work with mind and the world follows. It's so simple.

—**Byron Katie**

IT'S A MIND FIELD

The human mind: It's the best drama machine around. It's portable. It runs day and night, even, and especially, when we're not aware of it or paying attention. It is infinitely expandable and requires only imagination to operate. It cranks out some of the best stories around. Just feed it a few tidbits of hearsay, half-truths, some emotional charge, some childhood memories (the more traumatic, the better), and *voilà,* you're cooking, baby—with fire!

What you generate and experience depends entirely on what you feed your mind. Give the mind a story about terrorism in the country you're about to visit on vacation, and you've just generated a beautiful garden of fearsome delights complete with the image of being robbed at gunpoint as you're stepping away from an ATM. Feed it more stories of earthquakes, poverty, and a recent airline crash, and you're probably dialing the number of your travel agent to cancel the trip, muttering incessantly under your breath: *I ain't going nowhere!*

Factor in the effects of stress hormones cascading through your central nervous system, and "fearful" becomes more like a "fear fall." Once those chemicals get triggered in the brain, it can take some time to bring yourself back into balance.

I've had my share of excruciating meltdowns, of course, but none that I remember so vividly as the time, years ago, that I received an innocuous call from my daughter's middle school: "Your daughter was marked absent in homeroom today. Is she sick?"

I'm thinking: *I just put the kid on the bus.*

In the never-ending five minutes that I waited for the administrator to call me back, I went from complete equanimity—*just a simple error*—to imagining the absolute worst, most horrific scenario.

I felt the sickening feeling that parents have when they learn that their "baby" is missing. I felt the collective horror at the thought of inexplicable violations on a child. I felt my feeling so totally and completely that I was at the point of hyperventilating and on the verge of throwing up. I could not imagine living after this.

How did I go from zero to one hundred miles an hour in no time flat? In five minutes, I had gone on a whirlwind tour of my worst nightmare, based on nothing more than an innocent inquiry. It's amazing what the mind can do with very little data and evidence.

Still, as bad as it was to be pummeled by what felt like a category-five hurricane, a curious thing happened: I was aware of a part of me that stood by, witnessing the whole thing with no attachment. I watched as I went from complete calm to a madwoman ready to jump in my car and look for my daughter myself. I not only experienced but could *see* with my mind's eye the dark toxicity of this fear surging through my entire body as if a nuclear bomb had just exploded in my gut—a cancer in fast motion. I was aware of the intensity of these feelings and noted that if I allowed them to continue to cycle, unmitigated, through my body, it could do some serious damage over time.

The school administrator did call back to reassure me there had been a mistake. My daughter had been in another classroom making up a missed test. It took me more than an hour just to calm down after the call. I still felt sick, even though I knew that things were okay. I wanted to blame someone for how awful I felt, but I knew there was no one to blame, not even myself.

In the end, I realized that I had been given a huge gift. I was allowed to experience my worst nightmare without actually having to live it. I was given a chance to witness what the body does to process highly charged information that is fabricated in the head. I was given an opportunity to feel immense compassion for those who have had to go through nightmares of this kind in their own lives.

What I gained from this jolting experience—yet another of the endless teachable moments—was an awareness of the awesome power we have as humans every moment of every day. If so little can create so much in the playground of the mind, what could happen if we exercised some self-restraint and changed its daily diet! What if we consciously reframed a negative attitude or belief just once a day? What if we allowed our feelings—of pain, grief, or fear—to be just feelings, without acting on them or feeding them with more of the same? What if we could just witness an eruption without taking it personally—or seriously? If more of us practiced not identifying with just one little drama once a day, how might that change us and, dare I say, our world?

One thing I can say for sure: There is no tool or device required to create the joyous, spacious, clutter-free life you yearn for that doesn't already come built in to this amazing package we call the human body and this elastic generator we call the human mind!

FEAR FALL

So what exactly was that explosion I felt in my gut? Why did it feel so visceral and incapacitating? Why did it affect me for so very long after the event had already passed?

If I were to retell my phone-call story from a (very simplified) biochemical perspective, the chain reaction might look something like this:

> The external trigger is a phone call from my daughter's middle school. A wave of fear creates a series of electrical impulses in my brain that signal my body to produce certain chemicals. Once fired, these stress chemicals flood my system seeking out receptor sites that specialize in dread and panic. As long as I remain in a high state of alert and keep feeding the fear, these molecules continue to reproduce and, worse, stick around. Like clutter.

It's not just the damage that makes an event like this so significant, but how it sets up a pattern that predisposes similar meltdowns the next time someone calls out of the blue, the evening news features a story about a missing child, or a black pickup truck with darkened windows passes by on the street.

This is one of the ways we get hooked in by our stories and even addicted to them. And how to avoid going into a fear fall? We practice not "going there"; we stop the destructive thought before it unleashes its chemical avalanche.

WHAT IS YOUR STORY?

As bestselling author Byron Katie says, our problems are not the cause of our suffering, but rather the *thinking* about our problems causes us pain. When we can recognize that all our physical and emotional clutter began first as a thought that we've latched on to, we can begin to dismantle it the same way it came: by releasing the charge and reframing the thought the moment it arises. You can begin now by watching the stories you spin and asking yourself if they are true or not.

Here is my top ten list of reasons we hold on—compiled after years of listening to women in my "Clearing Circle" support groups talk about how clutter shows up in their lives and makes them feel. Notice which ones resonate for you, press your buttons, or even spark a little humor. If you feel some weather coming through, of course, use the moment to breathe, observe, and let it pass.

I. SCARCITY THINKING: "Just in Case"

This is probably the number-one reason why we hold on. It comes from a deep-seated belief that there is not enough to go around, the future is not to be trusted, and that life is just plain hard. It's thoughts such as "What if I need this again?" or "I might miss vital information if I don't read every single one of these magazine clippings [from three years ago]" or "They might stop making this brand, so I better stock up." Sometimes these scarcity patterns arise from beliefs held and passed from generation to generation triggered by major events like the Great Depression. The survival patterns of our pioneering forebears continue to be very much alive in many of us, as seen by our little squirrel tendencies to hold on and store things just in case a swarm of locusts makes it impossible for us to venture outdoors.

If it isn't enough to recreate the scarcity pattern, for some of us we also get to torment ourselves (and others) with liberal doses of *"I told you so"* when the external reality proves our point. The next time you find yourself spinning overgeneralizations such as "See, I told you! I just knew we shouldn't have gotten rid of that computer, second bicycle, exercise machine [*read:* clothing rack], refrigerator, golf clubs . . . ," use it as an opportunity to stop, breathe, and repeat the phrase: "It is now safe for me to let this go."

2. SHELF LIFE: "It's Not Used Up Yet"

This holding pattern comes from the belief that all manner of things, people, and experiences have a shelf life *and* must continue to sit on the shelf for several decades until they are used up: "I want to get my money's worth," "I spent a fortune on this," "This is too good to go to Goodwill" are some of the ways it shows up. The truth is that things can long outlast the real need for them. One way out is to imagine others enjoying the thing and passing it forward until its natural lifecycle is complete.

3. SENTIMENTAL ATTACHMENTS: "This Reminds Me of . . ."

Some of us fear that letting go of the sweet reminders of our past will erase and nullify the good memories forever. It's things like the tattered quilt that reminds you of summers on Lake Champlain; the kids' art projects; the blurry and faded snapshots of people and places you don't even recognize. Perhaps knowing that good memories—as energy—can never be lost or erased (and "bad" memories can be a constant drain) might make it easier to keep (digitize) what makes your heart sing and release what does not. The Acid Test for Clearing in chapter 23 is a good place to start.

4. GUILT #1: "Aunt Dorothy (God Rest Her Soul) Would Kill Me"

This is a biggie for those of us who believe that we are honor bound to carry forth the traditions left by our beloved ancestors. The seventeenth-century wingback chair *must* be carefully and prominently displayed because Grandpa did it and his grandpa before him. Forget about the fact that it's painful to sit on and will crack under the weight of anyone over forty pounds. We live in terror that our dearly departed will actually pop out of their graves and grab us by the throat if they find out that we've sold their beloved treasures on eBay. Take a few photos to put in the album for future generations. Write a loving summary describing the item and what it has meant to your family. Of course, if *you* adore the thing, keep it. Repair it, display it, and enjoy it for *your* sake, not Aunt Dorothy's!

5. GUILT #2: "This Stuff Needs Me"

Some of us think of our things as members of the family. Giving away the old laptop is akin to giving up a child for adoption to some unknown, less capable foster parent who cannot possibly care for it as well as we have! "I can't possibly throw this away until I find the right home for it" is an excellent delay tactic, and for those of us with major control issues, this objection rests high in the pantheon of holding patterns. If this, or any control pattern, is one you can relate to, there is a terrific antidote: self-acceptance and compassionate self-care. Daily doses of it.

6. EMPTINESS: "If I Get Too Clear, There Will Be Nothing Left of Me"

Many of us live in fear that if we give up our things, a deep, black hole of emptiness will set in. What will become of me if I let this go? For some of us, the idea of giving up our stuff (a relationship, a job) is so incapacitating that you'd think we'd been stranded alone, chained, and naked on a deserted island. The feelings of loss run deep. If I've learned anything about this particular holding pattern, it is not a fear of lack but the weather of grief that can be so paralyzing. Here's the good news for those of you who feel these swells so acutely: letting go—slowly, gently—offers you the perfect opportunity to feel and heal the experience of loss. Honor and acknowledge the objects (behaviors, relationships) you are releasing. Thank them, bless them, acknowledge what they have meant to you. Creating a special ritual or altar of letting go can help soften the hardwiring. Reward each clearing effort by doing something that makes your heart sing.

7. AVOIDANCE: "I Don't Want to Have to Feel Those Feelings"

When we're too afraid to be alone with our feelings, we might choose a special brand of protective covering. Denial protects us from having to do the unthinkable and "go there." Besides becoming clutter control freaks, we might become motor-mouth talk-aholics. We might eat ourselves into a near coma-tose state just to avoid the nagging feeling of grief or loss. Pain medication, alcohol, drugs, sex, hoarding—these avoidance strategies that give us a false sense of security are deeper and more destructive forms of holding on. Memo to self: Start slow, allow your feelings, and exercise extreme self-care. Tell your-self that there is light at the end of the tunnel (even if you don't believe it).

8. VICTIMIZATION: "Poor Me"

Replaying old tapes of parental neglect or abuse, a loss of a job, or a painful divorce are great ways to stay stuck and derail any clearing effort. A "poor me" pattern is a self-fulfilling one and a hard one to break, too, because it is so easily fed by the monkey mind. The next time you're feeling stuck in a rut and sorry for yourself, try this: Express gratitude for one thing in your life that *is* working and watch what happens.

9. SENSE OF BELONGING: "Makes Me Feel Like I Fit In"

We often hang on to stuff because it gives us an inflated feeling of impor-tance: the torn-up t-shirt from the 1972 Rolling Stones concert that shows how hip you are; the dusty collection of literary classics (that haven't been opened in three decades) that prove how smart you are; the boyfriend you can't give up because he's handsome and cool—forget about the fact that he mis-treats and disrespects you. If you must, take a photo of it (them, him) and let it (them, him) go! Then use the photo in a ritual of letting go.

10. COLLECTIVE UNCONSCIOUSNESS: "If 'Everyone' Is Doing or Having It, then It Must Be Okay"

It's easy to go into denial when the collective culture supports a way of life that can be harmful or damaging to our bodies, homes, environments, and lives. If *everyone* eats fast food, then it must be okay. If everyone uses pesticides to make their lawns a perfect, weed-free green, then it must be okay. If everyone has a gas-guzzling SUV, then it must be okay. If everyone gets/does/has . . . Watch your own inclinations to do or have something that doesn't feel right to you. Just because someone else does it or has it, doesn't mean that it is healthful and supportive *for you*. Pay attention to and honor your feelings. Also beware of your inclinations to judge those who do it or have those things. Your judgments of them are just as harmful!

MENTAL CLUTTER DEFINED

Mental clutter is the incessant chatter generated by the small mind, or monkey mind. This is the domain of the resident ego, barking orders to assure its eternal comfort and safety.

Some faces of mental clutter:

◊ auto-pilot fears: "I should," "I can't," "I couldn't," "I shouldn't"

◊ negative stories you tell yourself; limiting beliefs; self-blame

◊ guilty conscience

◊ "poor me," feeling victim

◊ gossip

◊ overthinking, overanalyzing, overrationalizing

◊ motor-mouth chatter, posturing, incessant blathering, yammering, harping

CLEARING PRACTICE

This is another opportunity to tune in to some of the "static and noise" you might be carrying.

In your journal, begin by making a list of at least five limiting beliefs—for example, any thought or behavior that rattles, jangles, stirs, enrages, defeats, or saddens you on a routine basis.

Your list could look like this:

◊ I can't have (do, be) that.

◊ Nobody gets me.

◊ I can't let go.

◊ What a waste my life is.

◊ I get nothing accomplished.

◊ I'll never get there.

After you've compiled your list, notice if you feel a surge of heat, greater thirst, increased heart rate, a momentary pang. Do nothing but allow yourself to feel any weather that is stirred. Don't forget to . . . *stop and feel.*

CLEARING JOURNAL

Use the statements below to shine light on the stories you tell yourself. For greater effect (i.e., awareness and emotional release), focus on one story at a time and repeat the process for each one.

◊ One of the stories I tell myself that doesn't serve me anymore is _____

◊ This story makes me feel _____

◊ I know that this story is not true [no longer serves me] because _____

◊ It is safe to let go of this story because [*psst,* notice the part of you that does not feel so safe] _____

◊ What *is* true about me (and I would like to tell myself instead) is _____

6 EMOTIONAL CLUTTER

Please take responsibility for the energy
you bring into this space.
—Dr. Jill Bolte Taylor

What do famous cartoon characters, clouds, and strings have in common? Nothing at all, unless you're attending one of my workshops and watching me illustrate how emotional clutter shows up in our lives, how it affects us and our world, and what it means to clear it. In discussing emotional clutter, I use these unlikely metaphors because each highlights a different aspect of the problem. When you can recognize these aspects, you are already on your way to clearing this form of invisible clutter.

IT'S ALL ENERGY

Belleruth Naparstek probably said it best when she wrote: "When all is said and done, we are nothing but vibration in a sea of living, intelligent energy." Though clutter appears to us as solid matter, if we reduced it to its smallest discernible parts, it is nothing more than atomic particles with frequency and intensity or, as the famous yoga master Paramahansa Yogananda describes it in his teachings, "congealed light." Japanese scientist, Dr. Masaru Emoto, in his book *The Hidden Messages in Water,* puts it like this:

> You might think, *Existence is vibration? Even this table? This chair? My . . . body?* It is indeed difficult to believe that things that you

can pick up with your hands and examine—things like wood, rocks, and concrete—are all vibrating.

As wave patterns, energy moves and changes, ebbs and flows. It forms and unforms and *informs*. Matter is constantly changing back into energy and energy into matter. Energy holds no grudges. It doesn't care if you're having a bad day. It is neither good nor bad. It just is—pure potential, pure expression, pure attraction.

Like those weather maps you see on the evening news, some patterns of energy might register as calm and peaceful in certain areas in your home, workplace, and life, while others might reveal more agitated and unsettled "low pressure" systems. Your spaces can feel prickly, compressed, and charged, while others are smooth and coherent. It all depends on how you relate to them; that is, how spacious, observant, and detached you are.

CLUTTER GOES WITH US EVERYWHERE

Remember Pigpen, that adorable *Peanuts* cartoon character who walks around with a permanent cloud of dust? To the degree that we are carting around a lifetime of limiting beliefs, emotional attachments, and all those aspects in ourselves that we suppress, resist, and deny—also known as "shadow"—we're not all that different from that cute little guy. The bigger our shadow, the smoggier, denser, and, dare I say, not-so-cute this invisible "cloud."

To understand how our personal energy field can affect other people, places, and things, imagine that everything swirling in that cloud is a collection of *strings:* Each object that you don't use or love represents one string that tethers you to it. A painful memory that you have not healed or embraced equals a string. A negative thought equals another. Many negative thoughts, addictions, unmitigated fear, hoarding, painful memories—rehashed over and over again—equals a stringy, energetic mess.

Like large-scale static cling, this would mean that *all* our stringy attachments go with us everywhere we go. We sleep, eat, play, live, make love, and work with . . . our clutter! They become like another member of the family, one that we are feeding, housing, and lugging around. The cloud may not always be visible to us. Until we consciously reduce some of the smoggy build-up, this cloud will filter and affect everything we think about, everything we do, and everyone we meet.

Combine yours with everybody else's stringy clouds of perceptions and personal agendas, and the world begins to look and feel like one of those maps you see in airline magazines that show all those red swooping lines connecting different cities around the world.

And we wonder why we can feel so stuck, stressed, confused, and depressed, needing ever-greater amounts of alcohol, medications, and escape tactics to calm down our short-circuiting nervous systems!

STICKY ENERGY

At the risk of sounding like one of those late-night infomercials, *But wait, there's more.* The thing about our Pigpen cloud is that it doesn't just travel with us everywhere we go. This cloud of clutter has two other distinguishing features:

◊ It has a powerful magnetic field that attracts more *strings* like it to itself;

◊ It leaves behind an energetic trail of unprocessed emotional debris that affects everyone else, people's living spaces, and the environment at large.

Based on the Law of Attraction, which simply states that "like attracts like," we attract at the level that we vibrate, twenty-four/seven. If our cloud is vibrating at the level of "poor me" or "worry about money" or "fear of success," for instance, we will not only attract people, places, and things that carry the exact same frequencies in their energy fields, but we will likely also leave a signature trail of worry and fear as we go. When you consider how human thoughts and emotions can negatively impact our living spaces, perhaps you'll forgive the rather crass but affectionate expression I use to describe these distinctly sticky energetic signatures. I call them "human droppings."

To put this in perspective, the opposite is also true. If we are vibrating at the level of love, gratitude, generosity, forgiveness, spaciousness, nonattachment, balance, and joy, we will leave a higher vibrational trail behind which some might experience as clarity. If we are very spacious and completely unattached, having reached the first stages of enlightenment, we will likely leave no trail at all!

STRINGS ATTACHED

To see how emotions can affect us and our living spaces, imagine this scenario: Let's say you have a huge argument with your spouse and have not resolved, or cannot seem to resolve, the tension between you by feeling and releasing the emotional charge you two are holding. Energetic charge or polarity is like the plus and minus of a battery. The intensity of the argument and the length of time it has been festering work together to determine the degree of polarity that the charge holds.

If there was a lot of intensity to begin with, your fight will have left a nice-sized *dropping* in the space where you two had your argument. If you are still vibrating unhappiness and tension, there will likely be some *strings* connecting you to this spot and to each other.

Unbeknownst to either of you, along comes someone you don't even know who's also having a bad day. Because this third person's bad day is vibrating at the same frequency as your earlier fight, she might resonate with this particular field of disturbed energy (because of some unfinished business of her own [*read:* unloved parts of herself]), have a mini-meltdown, and leave her own stringy mess *right on top of yours!* If you haven't found a way to clear what you left there in the first place, you might find yourself tethered to the overlays of other people's unfinished business and bad days.

How do I know all this? As a longtime professional space-clearing practitioner, I am trained to tune in to myriad distinct metaphysical, geophysical, and electromagnetic energy signatures that swirl about in people's living spaces. I can feel the sticky residue of human emotions anchored in rooms, hallways, closets, furniture, and people's possessions. I can identify the disturbing influences of neighboring homes, battlegrounds, construction projects, underground water, cell towers—you name it—anything that may cause my clients to wonder why they can't sleep or why they're stressed, depressed, sad all the time, or broke. If you've ever walked into a space that doesn't feel good to you, a space that feels prickly or sluggish, hyped up, unfriendly, or just plain creepy, you'll know what I'm talking about.

If you're feeling a little daunted by the toxic implications of human unconsciousness on our quality of life and our living spaces, it might help to know that you have already begun to clear it by simply being more aware and taking responsibility for what you put out in the world.

Responsibility, as in the ability to respond.

STRING CLEANING

I had a houseguest once who gave me an unforgettable taste of what it's like to take *everything* with you after a visit. My friend, who practices living consciously, packed up all her belongings—that is, both her physical possessions and her energetic ones. The second she drove away, my house felt energetically completely clear, as if she had never been there! What remained were the good memories of a fun visit and her sheets to be washed. It was an astonishing effect, and one that you might not notice at all if it weren't for how most spaces feel—cluttered, heavy, stuck.

Because we are not separate from each other in the bigger scheme, clutter of all kinds affects our spaces and our lives, even if it's not ours. So, next time you notice an intense sensation or emotional squall that you weren't feeling moments before—like a headache or a heaviness in the chest or a sad thought—it is most likely not yours! Feel the feeling without identifying it as yours, and *move on!*

Be mindful of the stringy stuff you take with you or leave behind. The less identified you can be about any emotional weather you encounter, the easier it will be to call back what is yours, let go what is not yours, and snip away the energetic ties or *strings.* This is conscious clutter clearing at a very high level and you can begin now by noticing how you feel right this second. You can use all the chapters in part 4 to practice detaching with awareness.

YOU CAN'T TAKE IT WITH YOU, OR CAN YOU?

It's pretty obvious that we cannot take our savings account with us when we die. No pearl necklaces, no photo albums, no sports car. But who is to say that we don't carry our best (and worst) memories, passions, and attachments—as energy—with us to the next dimension when we pass on? If we're energy beings after all, isn't it reasonable to hypothesize that there is a part of us that goes on for the ride? Or even "sticks" around?

Years of experience have taught me that negative emotions held in a space links that space to the person who left it there until it is cleared, even if the person died years before! So when you think of ghosts, they are not actual people who are stalking their householders, but rather, highly charged negative thought patterns and memories left behind by people who likely suffered a hard and painful life.

If this seems far-fetched, allow me to share a story of what happened to me the week after I space cleared my home for the first time. I received an unexpected call from someone I had known casually from my yoga class. "You're not going to believe this, Stephanie," she said, almost out of breath, "but the house you live in was *my* house for fourteen years!" My friend was looking for my phone number in the directory and was surprised to see her old address pop up under my name. She had raised her three kids in this house. The wood-burning stove we inherited was the same one she had had installed. The tulips and the peonies that we enjoy every spring were her gifts to the place.

During our conversation, I learned that my friend had suffered an inexplicable stomach ailment and intense release on the very day that I had cleared the house. She told me that this "release" appeared to have come out of nowhere and led to her feeling noticeably lighter and significantly more energized afterward.

Coincidence? It's impossible to say for sure if the mysterious weather that moved through her body rather suddenly could have been the result of a conscious cleansing of my home.

Whatever your belief in the invisible or in the hereafter may be, perhaps just knowing the potential effects that our thoughts can have on a space might inspire you to clear, clear, clear—with awareness—right now, while you are able to lighten your load and make a difference. When you clear your clutter by acknowledging how it feels and detaching from your drama, you make it possible to move on—or pass over—with a cleaner slate. Everyone wins!

AS WITHIN, SO WITHOUT

If everything you've read so far is making your head spin, just breathe, notice any weather that is being stirred, and take a moment to imagine.

In the light of this quote by Anaïs Nin, "We don't see things as they are, we see them as we are," imagine what the world might look and *feel* like to you when you are not carting around so much physical, mental, and emotional *stuff*.

Imagine the kinds of people, places, and life experiences that you might attract if you vibrated and magnetized at higher levels.

Imagine the massive difference you could make by simply choosing to show up and move through life in a lighter, more conscious way.

All it takes is your willingness to accept, allow, and . . . be aware.

EMOTIONAL CLUTTER DEFINED

Emotional content, by nature, has an up and down quality to it and, as we have seen, shows up in two significant ways: as sticky energetic attachments (aka *strings*) that bind people and things to each other and go with us everywhere we go, and as highly charged stress patterns (aka *droppings*) with a strong magnetic field that stick to the environment. Both forms of imbalance will attract more of themselves if not cleared. Left untended, highly charged thoughts and emotions can wreak havoc on other unsuspecting beings, our living spaces, and our world at large.

Some faces of emotional clutter are:

◊ reactions, polarizing opinions, pressed buttons

◊ holding grudges

◊ taking things personally

◊ constant worry and fear

◊ temper tantrums, emotional meltdowns

- ◊ road rage, ranting
- ◊ addictions to food, alcohol, drugs, sex, the Internet, etc.; bingeing, hoarding

CLEARING PRACTICE
TUNING IN TO EMOTIONAL CHARGE

Below is an exercise to tune in to some of the "static" you might be carrying. Take your index card and again cover the list of sentences below. Uncover one at a time and read or say it out loud, noticing what happens. Remember, whatever you gather here is just another data point.

- ◊ S/he feels toxic.
- ◊ I can't stand not knowing.
- ◊ It's hopeless.
- ◊ I can't let go.
- ◊ It hurts.
- ◊ I'm afraid for _____.

Stop and feel.

CLEARING JOURNAL

Use the statements below to tune in to the emotional clutter in your life. [*Psst,* if it's of any comfort, know that simply bringing awareness to emotional charge helps to clear it—*for good!*]

- ◊ Some of the beliefs that create stuckness in my life and keep me spinning more *strings* are _____
- ◊ It is safe for me to release these stringy attachments because _____
- ◊ One behavior in myself that I'd like to release is _____
- ◊ One thing I can do right now [today] to feel better is _____
- ◊ Some of the shifts in myself that I have noticed since I began being more aware are _____

7

FEEL TO HEAL

All great discoveries are made by those
whose feelings run ahead of their thinking.
—C. H. Parkhurst

One afternoon as I was working at my desk, someone came to my front door soliciting financial support for some rather hazy scholarship fund. The kid seemed friendly enough, shaking my hand and acting as if we were old friends. Deep down in my bones I *smelled* a scam. It was disarming that he knew my name and said that my neighbor had sent him. I managed to finesse a quick retreat and get back to my writing. I wouldn't have thought much of this encounter except that for an hour afterward, I felt really off center, jangled, and just plain icky. My normally positive frame of mind felt contaminated somehow, opened up to a wave of intense weather that seemed to come out of the blue.

Or shall we say "blues." What flooded over me suddenly and out of nowhere was my inner critic going on a wild rampage of bashing everything I had been doing that afternoon. If I had not paid attention to the signals I was receiving from my body and the unnerving nonsense that my mind was spewing out, I might have allowed this one event to take over and ruin my day.

Instead, I caught and stopped it. In the moment that I could see that the emotional weather I was experiencing was *not mine* but my body processing the disturbing effects of an encounter at my front door, I was able to switch gears and move on.

I also found myself smiling at how the universe delivers these "this is only a test" freebies just when I need to make a point. The point being, of course, in case it's not yet immediately obvious: It pays to "follow your knows."

THE BODY KNOWS

If you have tried any of the clearing practices presented so far, you may have noticed that your body, with its extraordinary sensing capabilities of smell, touch, sight, hearing, taste, and inner knowing, can be a key source for a wealth of information.

Unfortunately, most of us tend to shut down or dismiss this amazing resource and rely mostly on the intellect to provide us with the vital information we need to carry us from day to day. Every time we second guess ourselves, we are allowing the mind to call the shots . . . again.

If you consider that this intelligence comes through the murky filters of our past—our conditioning, fears, judgments, and attachments—you can see how its reliability for delivering pure, clear information can be mighty questionable.

There is no better way to clear than to invite your thinking mind to step aside and allow your feelings to be your guide.

Without the body, you cannot sniff out the places in your home that are really stuck. Without the body, you cannot sense a potentially harmful situation. Without the body, you cannot experience the full effect of weather patterns to show you where you hold on. The thing about the body is that it has a way of sussing out holding patterns in an instant, ones that the noisy mind cannot even touch (literally).

CLEARING IS FEELING

It is important to clarify that feeling as a vehicle for clearing is not the same as emoting. Feeling is not an expressive act but an ability to open up the channels that *allow* information—be it highly charged or not—to simply pass through us.

Feeling requires a level of detachment. Though this may seem oddly paradoxical, what you will learn in the coming chapters is that there is a quality of *witnessing* in the feeling process that differs greatly from the more familiar emotional venting or reacting. Feeling is a way that we respond to information from our environment.

Responding opens up our channels; reacting shuts them down.

So, when you are asked to "feel your feelings" as part of the clearing process in this book, what it means exactly is this:

1. **Allow** any weather—be it stormy or clear—to pass through to the extent that you can handle it.

2. **Experience** this information through your physical and nonphysical senses. If it's clammy hands, notice them. If it's resistance, experience it. If it's nausea, allow it. If it's tears, shed them. If it's shame, embrace it.

3. And finally (this is key), **Don't Identify,** own, or take any of it personally. Allow it to be a passage of weather as information and feedback, nothing more.

Feelings are the only true indicator of where we are open to our deepest desires and where we close down. Pure joy and effortless ease, for example, would be an indicator of complete alignment. Pure conflict and unease, would not. Pretty simple, when you think about it.

FOLLOW YOUR KNOWS

Humans are like radios that receive and transmit information, as energy, all the time. The body's sophisticated sensing capabilities are the antennae and processing center for all the signals we receive and send out. Sensations (called feelings in this book) give us the means to read and interpret these signals.

Though we can count on all of our senses to pick up information from our environment, many of us have one or two senses with which we tend to lead. For example, I have a highly developed sense of smell. I can smell things before I can see them. I can smell gas leaks that most might not. I can smell cigarette smoke from smokers in passing cars, even if their windows are rolled up! I can even smell stress patterns *(droppings)* that have been left behind by previous occupants in homes for decades. I can smell energetic "off gassing" when I am clearing a person or being cleared.

What senses do you use the most? Try this little acid test, and 〇〇〇 help you identify one or several senses with which you might typical〇 When you're talking casually with someone, which of these phrases are y〇 most likely to use?

◊ I *know* what you mean.

◊ I *see* what you mean.

◊ I *hear* what you're saying.

◊ I *feel* what you're saying.

◊ I'm *touched.*

◊ I can just *taste* it.

◊ I can *visualize* it.

◊ I can *smell* it a mile away.

◊ I *smell* trouble.

◊ I can just *imagine* that.

As you embark on your clearing journey, accept your body as one of your most highly developed sources of undeniable information. Notice the ways that you typically tune in to receive, read, and transmit signals from your environment. Notice if you are more likely to get a visual image, an auditory sound, or a kinesthetic knowing. Having this awareness can help you sniff out the places in your home that don't feel very good or feel stuck. It can help you tune in to people's true motivations and assess whether they serve your highest good or not. It can help you detach more readily from disturbing sensations that are *not yours,* and were never yours to begin with. Adopting a regular, daily clearing practice using the exercises in this book can help you develop your awareness and sensing abilities even further.

CLEARING PRACTICE
TUNING IN TO THINGS

When we live our lives on automatic pilot, we lose touch with the things and activities that make our hearts sing—and cringe. Here's an opportunity

experience to see what "vibe" you get. Remember that

ong, good or bad answer to this exercise. Someone's

ce of harmony could be someone else's perception and

bottom line is that you have a tangible experience of

nt patterns of energy—both valuable teachers that can

formed choices in your life.

ere is nothing to "do" with these simple exercises. Just

smell, touch, sight, taste, hearing, inner knowing) to

speak for ... nd shed light for you. Be your own silent witness.

1. **Choose:** Pick one small object that you love (*read:* love madly, adore, makes your heart sing!) and one small object that you do not love or use (aka clutter).

2. **Tune In:** Place the object of clutter behind you and hold the object you love in front of you. Fully "be" with the object you love, using all of your senses. What is the vibe you get? Notice your body as it holds this object. Notice your thoughts and beliefs about this object without identifying with them. What information can you glean from just "being" with this?

3. **Switch and Repeat:** When you feel complete, place the object you love behind you and bring forward the object of clutter. Repeat the above steps.

4. **Compare:** When you have completed this task, place both objects side by side in front of you. Can you feel the energetic difference between the two as you sense one and then the other? Record all sensations in your clearing journal.

CLEARING JOURNAL

Take this opportunity to reflect on your experience of sensing the things that please you and those that do not.

◊ The big differences that I noticed when I tuned in to each of the objects were _____

◊ This data came through primarily from my sense of [choose one or more that applies: smell, touch, sight, hearing, taste, and inner knowing] _____

◊ One thing I can do right now [today] that would support me is _____

◊ An uncomfortable feeling I had recently that I can now see was *not* mine was _____

8
TUNE IN

Move closer, lean in, get curious; even for
a moment, experience the feelings
without labels, beyond being good
or bad. Welcome them. Invite them.
Do anything that helps melt the resistance.

—**Pema Chödrön**

How's it going?

When people ask me this question in passing, my first impulse is to tell them my whole story, even though I know they're just being polite and friendly. They don't really want to know:

- ◊ I couldn't sleep last night.
- ◊ My coffee tasted old this morning—and p.s., where is the nearest Starbucks?
- ◊ I'm sick of always having to clean up after everyone.
- ◊ I haven't worked out in days, and I feel like a whale.
- ◊ I'm famished and cranky.
- ◊ What was I thinking to wear these shoes . . . my feet are killing me.
- ◊ Darn, I wished that I had bought that jacket I saw on sale yesterday. I can't believe I let that one go.

◊ Will this pain that I feel in my knees ever stop?

◊ I can't deal with everyone's whining.

I'll usually retort with my own equally non-present, fake-happy *Good!* (with the little lilt on the top of it), just to move things along.

That's me living on autopilot.

So how do you respond in a way that feels more authentic, especially when you're in a hurry and you have a million things swirling around in your head?

What if the next time someone asked you how you were "doing," you could move past the stories (that no one really asked to hear anyway) and go directly to tuning in to *the feeling beneath the story?* To use the connection with the person as an opportunity to quietly check in with yourself and allow whatever it is you're feeling to arise—without (and this is key) judging it or doing anything to fix it.

What makes this exercise one of the most basic and powerful in *my* world of clearing is this:

◊ It takes only seconds of your time.

◊ You become more present with yourself.

◊ You become more available to the person you're talking to.

◊ You become more present with your surroundings.

◊ You can clear tension by simply observing and feeling it.

◊ You become more discerning about how and where you spend your time in general.

◊ You become more discerning about whom you choose to hang out with (i.e., someone who makes you feel good).

Awareness. It changes everything. *Responding* from a place of awareness changes everything.

CLEARING PRACTICE
TUNING IN TO RIGHT NOW

Close your eyes. Take a nice, easy breath in, then a slow, emptying breath out. Take a few moments to breathe out all thought and tension and breathe in pure awareness and possibility.

When you feel centered, notice and *allow* how you are feeling at this moment. Using any of the prompts below, do a full-body scan from the top of your head to the tips of your toes.

Notice and allow all sensations, thoughts, emotions. If you feel like you cannot shake off an annoyance, a grudge, or a burden, just notice *that*.

Body

◊   Is it tight and contracted? If so, where exactly?

◊   How's your breathing? Is it shallow? Is it full and relaxed?

◊   Is your mouth dry? Are you thirsty?

◊   Do you notice other sensations: heart rate change, a knot in your stomach, sweaty palms, joint pain, fatigue, anything else?

◊   Are you tired, yawning, zoning out, bored? Or are you feeling attentive, energized, excited?

Thoughts

◊   Do you feel foggy-headed or clearheaded?

◊   Are you analyzing, criticizing, chatty, in task mode?

◊   Are you chewing on a thought or worrying about something or someone?

◊   Are you spinning another round of woulda-coulda-shouldas?

Emotions

◊   Do you feel a pang of something—sadness, grief, fear?

◊   Are you holding a grudge?

◊   Did someone press your button? If so, where in your body do you feel it?

◊   Do you feel grumpy or annoyed? If so, what does grumpiness or annoyance feel like? Is it heavy, tight, contracting, achy, congesting?

◊   Do you feel stressed, overwhelmed, fried?

◊   Are you feeling reactive, rattled, jangled, off-balance, nauseous, suddenly ill?

When you feel complete, open your eyes and notice how you're feeling now. Notice if you feel the same or different from how you did when you started the exercise.

CLEARING JOURNAL

Complete the following statements [*psst*, remember, the trick here is to notice whatever comes into your awareness without resisting it. You may notice that by simply being a witness, any discomfort you feel might shift more quickly into something that feels better—or even good].

◊ Before the clearing practice I was feeling _____

◊ What comes up when I allow myself to feel is _____

◊ It is safe for me to allow all feelings because _____

◊ Some of the sensations that I tend to feel the most are an indicator of _____

◊ Some shifts, synchronicities, or dreams that I've experienced since I began my clearing journey include _____

AWARENESS

Clutter comes in many forms and has many faces: It is visible and invisible; it is a symptom of imbalance called "weather"; it is the limiting beliefs that cloud who we are; it is stuck energy.

Anytime our buttons get pressed by a person, place, or issue, it means that we are holding a charge.

Witnessing (by feeling) the weather without attachment releases charge.

The human mind is a powerful generator that cannot be turned off; it can only be directed.

Fear creates stress chemicals that flood the body and affect its chemistry.

Energy holds no grudges; it doesn't care if we're having a bad day.

Strings are sticky energetic attachments that bind people and things to each other; they go with us everywhere and will increase in number until they are cleared.

Droppings are highly charged stress patterns that stick to the environment; they have a strong magnetic field and attract more of themselves if not cleared.

Most of the stress we feel is not ours; it becomes "ours" the moment we identify with it.

The body offers the finest physical and nonphysical capabilities to tune in and receive guidance.

Awareness changes everything.

PART II

INTENTION
SHIFT THE FOCUS

When you change the way you look at things,
the things you look at change.
—Dr. Wayne Dyer

9 CLEARING WITH INTENTION

It's never too late to choose optimism, to choose action, to choose excellence. The best thing is that it only takes a moment—just one second—to decide.
—**Seth Godin**

WHERE THE MIND GOES, ENERGY FLOWS

The mind is like a toddler with a short attention span who goes after anything interesting and reachable. After a few minutes, she's bored and goes on to the next thing. Without her parents' constant attention, a toddler will go after stuff that isn't exactly in her highest interest—the kitchen knife, ongoing traffic, the Drano under the bathroom sink. Similarly, without mindfulness—that quality of bringing awareness to our thoughts and feelings without judging them as good or bad—our mind can easily turn to negative images, doom-and-gloom predictions, gossip, endless chatter.

Living and clearing consciously means pulling the toddler back *every* time she goes off on another one of her many excursions. Be it a tailspin of worry or self-doubt, our job is to reel in the *strings* and send them in a new, more positive direction.

Again and again and again.

This super-elastic thing we call the mind can be a powerful vehicle for your purposes in clearing clutter. Like a toddler, the mind is actually relatively easy to redirect, if you're willing to mind it and not confuse it with mixed messages.

The "kid" might throw some tantrums, but with practice and patience, she's capable of blazing new trails that are infinitely more joyous, uncomplicated, and clear.

CLEARING WITH INTENTION

Clearing with intention is a way to get your higher self—the part of you that is infinitely aware—to communicate with the toddler mind, continuously steering her in the direction of your heart's longing. It is also more than simply directing or guiding your thoughts purposefully. As the full-throttle engine of a powerful manifesting machine, your intentions cannot be understated. There are two caveats, however:

1. **Be clear how you state, invoke, visualize, and feel your intentions.** The engine, once fired up, will produce results! If you are visualizing and feeling more financial abundance in your life that is encoded with a sense of optimism, possibility, and expansiveness, the universe will respond in kind. If, on the other hand, you are sending a signal for more abundance, which is laced with worry, scarcity, or neediness, the universe *will respond to the scarcity signals* by giving you more scarcity. In short, it is the quality of feeling that you send out that delivers what you get.

2. **Let go of attachment to the outcome.** Results don't always come in the package or form that you might expect. By holding tightly to an agenda, an expectation, or a timetable, you close doorways that could lead you to places you never imagined. Your sole job here is to express (feel) your intention and get out of the way!

The stories, clearing practices, and journal exercises in part 2 will give you lots of practice tuning in and redirecting your thoughts with clarity and spacious detachment. Short or long, may each chapter remind you to slow down and keep it simple—always.

10   IN TEND

Once you make a decision,
the universe conspires to make it happen.
—**Ralph Waldo Emerson**

I know of no handbook that shows us how to deconstruct and reshape a life, no natural, follow-the-dot sequence that takes us gently by the hand from point A to B. There was definitely no user's manual when I quit teaching at the height of a successful twenty-year career.

If you read the preface to this book, you'll know a bit about how I came into this clearing business. In it, I share how I went from being a professional *somebody* with benefits to a jobless nobody—on purpose.

What I didn't share is *how* exactly things began to shift for me; how the universe conspired to help me move forward into a whole new direction that my higher self was no doubt orchestrating behind the scenes. In almost imperceptible whispers, the clues arrived in the form of an innocent query and the unexpected gift of a book.

These pivotal encounters that galvanize us have a way of sneaking in the back door. In the first of these two encounters, I was asked at a party if I had a business card. I'm thinking *Business card? Me?*

But this innocuous request did something to me. It unleashed a host of unexpected and energizing possibilities. *Hmmm . . . a business card.* The question challenged me to consider what my card would say if I had one to give out to people. It tapped into the place that knew all along: my heart. *Tending the Home . . . Nourishing Homes . . . Beautiful Home Spaces . . . Healing Home . . . Feeling at Home . . .* The phrases flickered on and off like little neon signs as my mind scanned the airwaves for answers to what my ideal life and new identity might look and feel like. It felt really good to play with new ideas, to wake up to possibility. All that aimless floating that I had experienced up to this point in my unpaid sabbatical suddenly felt like directed floating.

It's a simple exercise. Give the brain one question to chew on, and it can take you places you never imagined possible. Massaging sentence fragments to design my tagline had a delicious way of connecting the dots of my life that spanned forty-plus years of experience, beginning with my love of creating beautiful home spaces when I was a child and my exploration of metaphysical ideas as a teenager. The business card question took me as far back as I could remember and revealed a whole new direction that I was quietly and unknowingly cultivating. Things began to make some sense.

Just days after this big moment of clarity, the second pivotal encounter happened: a book about clearing spaces was delivered, unbidden, to my front door by someone I barely knew. "Thought this might interest you," read the accompanying note. It still amazes me how I get what I need when I need it.

If the business card exercise was like receiving a special key, my being offered a book about space clearing felt like being shown the doorway to which the key offered special entry. This one gateway would lead me down a path to the next threshold, then the next, revealing new openings only when I was ready to understand and live them. These pathways covered a lot of ground and were not always comfortable or easy. But they took me places that I could never have planned or predicted, even if I had tried.

CLEARING PRACTICE
IN TENDING

Here is an opportunity to illuminate and "tend" to your soul's deepest stirrings. On a piece of paper or in your journal, take a few minutes to design a business card logo, with a tagline that expresses how you wish to be identified and reflects an aspiring "new you."

Don't think too hard. Just allow your highest and best self to inform you. When you feel complete, follow up by filling in the clearing journal statements below.

Have fun with this! Notice how it feels before, during, and afterward. Notice if, and how, it energizes you. Record any surprises that come out of this simple practice.

CLEARING JOURNAL

In your journal, take a moment to reflect on the following.

◊ *Ta-dah! Welcome to the NEW "me"!* (which I can best describe right now as _____)

◊ Some of the ways I can actively realize this powerful new me are _____

◊ It feels really good to home in on my deepest yearnings and desires because _____

◊ As I tend to my inner life (in tend), I notice these whispers [signs, glimmers] coming through: _____

ACT AS IF

We are not meant to be perfect; we're meant to be whole.
—Jane Fonda

After our daughter was born and it was clear that we had outgrown our cozy home in the city, my husband and I began the process of looking for a new place in a quieter, less urban community. We had no idea where the search would land us. For fun, we would take weekend drives into neighborhoods we loved, even if they were out of state or out of our price range. We would photograph Victorian homes on quiet, tree-lined streets because these captured the essence of what we loved most and where we dreamed about living one day. The photos would then go into our "ideal image" album. Without getting too attached to the neighborhoods or falling into deep funks over the fact that most of these places were out of our reach, we simply allowed ourselves to enjoy and act as if we lived someplace like that. I would imagine my car in the driveway. I would pick the window that would be our bedroom. I would consider the colors I might choose to repaint the façade.

A couple of years later, we were invited one day to have lunch at the home of a friend about twenty miles west of us. Her house was in a small town that we had not considered before and knew almost nothing about. The streets, lined with mature oak and maple trees and graceful century-old Victorian homes, were spacious and welcoming. The houses looked almost identical to a neighborhood we had photographed in a whole other state two years before!

There was even a "For Sale" sign that caught our eye on the front lawn of a cute house that turned out to be within our price range. On that day, we realized that this town was a real possibility for us. Within about six months, we found ourselves living in the house of our dreams. It was clear to us that we had manifested this place by holding a strong intention of what we wanted and a vision of what could be.

There's no big secret to this envisioning thing. If your heart's desire is to live in a clear, clean, peaceful home, surrounded by nothing but beautiful plants, you can begin by cutting out pictures in magazines that reflect that spacious quality. You can bring home fresh flowers or a plant to remind you. If you yearn for a life partner, you can begin by visualizing this person and maybe even emptying out a drawer or two or buying an extra toothbrush to attract this possibility.

Creating an image of what you want your life to look and feel like before, during, or after you have cleared your clutter is a powerful message to send to the unconscious mind. The unconscious doesn't know the difference between reality and the ideal image. By surrounding yourself with the energetic signature of these images, the unconscious will begin to organize a whole new reality based on these powerful intentions. It is doing so right now, in fact, just by reading these words!

CLEARING PRACTICE

Re-creating a more spacious vision for yourself is like developing a new muscle. Because positive images alone hold a very high vibration, they become very attractive and a powerful reminder of what is possible. It's also a lot of fun to pretend you have already manifested your deepest dreams. Remember that focusing on the absence of a quality (i.e., the fear of not getting it or the reasons why it might not come to pass) is equally effective—for delivering *negative* results—so try to relax the fearful mind as much as possible. You can stay positive and focused by bringing to consciousness only that which you desire and by reining in the toddler mind when it goes off again in the opposite direction.

ENVISIONING

Here are some ways to practice flexing this muscle [*psst,* remember to have fun with this and let go of your attachment to the outcome!]:

◊ **Clarify:** Photograph people's homes, streets, yards, babies, cars, etc., and place them where you are likely to see them a lot: your screensaver, refrigerator, car, bathroom mirror, "ideal image album." Replace or change the images when you feel that they have gone stale, or you no longer notice them.

◊ **Dream Big:** Display a photo of someone who inspires you or someone who has defied huge odds to reach unimaginable heights of success and personal power, such as Oprah Winfrey, John Lennon, or Nelson Mandela.

◊ **Feel Rich:** Get one hundred one-dollar bills out of the bank and scatter them all over the floor or your bed and throw them up in the air as if you have just hit the jackpot.

◊ **Sell:** Prominently display a photograph of the house you are trying to sell with a big "Sold" sign across the front. You can add *"Sold! For more than the asking price!!"* at the bottom if you wish.

◊ **Attract:** Empty a drawer, buy a toothbrush, make a second set of keys to attract your life partner. Buy a baby outfit or toy to attract a baby into your life, or have someone photograph you with a baby in your arms.

CLEARING JOURNAL

After you've completed one or more of the practices above (or your own variation), take a moment to reflect on what you most desire. Even if nothing inspires you yet, take time to write in your journal anyway. Sometimes just writing down what makes you feel stuck will create openings and trigger a new idea.

◊ What I most desire right now is _____

◊ It is super easy and fun for me to "act as if" because _____

◊ Envisioning what I most desire makes me feel [*psst,* notice any resistance] _____

◊ One simple thing that I can do today [every day this week] to attract what I most desire is _____

12   BE GRATEFUL

If the only prayer you said in your whole life
was "thank you," that would suffice.
—**Meister Eckhart**

Wondering what a one-minute practice of conscious gratitude might look like, I posed it as a question to myself one morning before getting out of bed. What popped up was the directive to "thank everything."

So I did—in that *Goodnight Moon* children's book sort of way. I began by thanking everything I experienced for a whole minute as I did what I usually do to get ready for my day:

> Thank you, body, for letting me sleep through the night (without having to get up and pee once). Thank you, bed, for being so yummy and cozy. Thank you, underwear, for being on sale when I bought you. Thank you, arms and legs, for being able to function so that I *can* get dressed. Thank you, squeak-in-the-closet-door, for reminding me to be grateful. Thank you breath . . .

I was on a roll. My one minute turned out to be more like five minutes. Here's what I noticed when I contemplated the practice later in the day:

◊   I was more present.

◊   I appreciated things that I usually take for granted.

◊   I had not done what I routinely do when I open my closet door, which is to scold myself for not having fixed the squeak.

◊ I never once judged my body.

◊ I felt really good.

Gratitude and clearing. They go hand in hand.

GRATITUDE IS CLEARING

It may be true that there is no such thing as a quick fix in this clearing adventure, but if I've learned anything at all, it is that being grateful for everything, all the time, can change the vibration of clutter and produce miracles! As Melody Beattie shares so beautifully in *The Language of Letting Go Journal:*

> Gratitude unlocks the fullness of life. It turns what we have into enough, and more. It turns denial into acceptance, chaos to order, confusion to clarity. It can turn a meal into a feast, a house into a home, a stranger into a friend. . . . Gratitude makes sense of our past, brings peace for today, and creates a vision for tomorrow. Gratitude makes things right.

Gratitude ranks way up there on the list of ways to cultivate a more spacious life. As energy that is attractive, creative, and transformative, expressing appreciation is pure gold for how it can change your life on a dime. And it costs nothing but a little mindful attention.

Don't take my word for it. Try it. Make a list of the things that might give you pause or make you groan or recoil. Perhaps it's a case of adult-onset acne, the bills that keep piling up, the neighbor who plays her music too loud, or the army of ants that invades your kitchen every spring. Express your appreciation for these things in your life. Welcome them like old friends.

See if by shifting the focus you notice something you hadn't before. For example, when I began to name all the ants in my kitchen "Beto" (for no particular reason other than I liked that name, and it sounded like *vete,* which means "go away" in Spanish), I began to have a different relationship with them. They didn't bug me as much anymore, and, believe it or not, they stopped coming in droves. In fact, come to think of it, they're not coming around at all anymore.

I now notice that if I extend a kind greeting to a telemarketer instead of hanging up on him or her, I don't feel so jangled afterwards. I have also noticed that these calls have all but stopped! So have the store catalogues that used to inundate our mailbox. When we release the charge we hold around certain people, things, or issues, they fall away.

Giving thanks has a way of magically reducing the charge we hold around things and people. It stops the endless cycle of negativity and releases the offending *string*. Putting a positive spin on everything may be cause for incessant teasing by your cynical friends, but let's face it, this trait is very attractive and will attract more positive energy.

Adopt a daily mantra of "thank you." Thank the bus driver, the waitress, the mail carrier, the flight attendant, the pilot. Thank your teachers, doctors, store clerks, co-workers. Be grateful for the food you eat, the clothes you wear, the bed you sleep in. Appreciate your family. Acknowledge the miracle of your body to seek balance. Thank the universe for all the support you get (most of which we aren't even aware of) and for giving you opportunities to grow. Be grateful for your life. And if you find it's too hard to do sometimes, act as if you're grateful. Fake it and feel the resistance that it stirs.

So what are you grateful for? What do you notice when you name and feel your gratitude? What do you notice when you practice the meditation below?

CLEARING PRACTICE
APPRECIATING

Here are two ways to adopt a daily practice in appreciation:

You can begin right this second with a running one-minute commentary of what you are grateful for, what feels good, what works in your life, what you love.

If you feel a whine or a complaint coming on, catch yourself, snap yourself out of it with a phrase like "strike that" or "stop it," and reframe the thought with something more uplifting and positive. For example "I'm late" could be turned around to "I made it!"

See if by shifting the focus on the idea of *having* rather than lacking, you observe something you hadn't noticed before. If this exercise brings up some charge, take it as a sign to stop and feel.

Alternatively, you can deepen your experience of gratitude and quiet the mind by adopting the meditation described below and following up with the reflections in your clearing journal.

ATTITUDE OF GRATITUDE MEDITATION

If you do nothing else to further your quest for a lighter home and a clearer life, go for this simple daily practice. It was inspired by and adapted from a simple, nondenominational meditation technique I learned years ago from a group of monks called the Ishayas when I was living in Mexico.

It goes like this:

1. **Find** a comfortable place to sit.

2. **Close** your eyes and take a nice, easy breath in, then a slow, emptying breath out. Continue to breathe deeply until you feel very relaxed.

3. **Insert** this first phrase into your awareness: "Thank you, _____ [fill in with your own concept of the Divine or your idea of a higher power—which could be anything or anyone and can change over time], for my home."

4. **Allow** your thoughts to come and go, and notice what it feels like.

5. **Repeat** the same phrase if you wish, or **move on** to the next one: "Thank you, _____, for my body."

6. **Notice** your thoughts again. Notice any tightness or resistance in your body. Notice your breathing.

7. **Repeat** the final phrase: "Thank you, _____, for my life."

8. **Go easy.** Avoid the tendency to move too fast.

9. **Open** your eyes when you feel complete. Take a nice, easy breath in, then a slow, emptying breath out. Wiggle your fingers and toes.

10. **Write** down your reflections by following the prompts in the clearing journal below.

CLEARING JOURNAL

After you've had a chance to practice the Attitude of Gratitude Meditation, take a moment to complete the following.

◊ Some of the sensations that I notice and feel in my body when I express gratitude are _____

◊ What goes through my mind when I express gratitude is _____

◊ How and why it is easy for me to be grateful for everything is _____

◊ Ways that I can adopt an attitude of gratitude more regularly into my life are _____

BLESS AND RELEASE

13

*A symbolic or ceremonial experience is real
and affects one as much as an actual event.*
—Robert A. Johnson

The first time I space-cleared my own home, I discovered to my horror that I was a clutter-holic of the silent and hiding kind. My house had always been neat as a pin, organized, *and* jammed beyond capacity with stuff. For all of you out there who think us "tidy types" are some kind of superhuman *wunderkind,* you may be relieved to know that being organized and being clear are not always the same—at least not in my case. It was time for me to look at my own stuff and the reasons behind my toxic squirrel tendencies.

One fall weekend, my husband and I had the brilliant idea of pulling down all the boxes that contained twenty years of our respective professional lives. For me, it was countless cardboard boxes of every quiz, test, paper topic, and syllabus that I had ever assigned to my high school students. I had even saved multiple copies of these "just in case" I needed an extra set. I had assignments that had been mimeographed with purple ink, typed on a standard typewriter, and stuck together with rusty old paperclips. The hundreds of these paperclips looked like a small mountain when I finished! The amount of stuff I had saved was staggering, dating back to 1976 when I had begun my teaching career.

It took all afternoon and the next afternoon as well. Boxes and bags of paper began to line our sidewalk for the recycling truck that comes by each week. All the physical evidence of my teaching career went into those bags.

When the recycling truck came around a few days later, I watched as the Trash God lifted each and every sack. I put my shaky hands together in a prayerful gesture of gratitude and blessing as I watched the entire contents of my former life depart forever. I didn't know about *strings* back then, I just felt light beyond words! I floated for days afterward.

A few hours had passed when I ran into an acquaintance who mentioned casually that she was selling her small upright piano. She wanted to move it fast, so she was offering it at a good price. *Hmmm. A piano.* My wheels began to turn. So this is what it means to make space. Sometimes we don't know what we're making room for, and it can be interesting to see what shows up when you're not expecting anything. I didn't really know it at the time, but we had just created space for music to come into our lives. We had also created space for new friendships. The people who sold us the piano have since become some of our dearest friends.

THE POWER OF RITUAL

If you think of dreams as the way that your unconscious mind communicates to you in special symbolic code while you sleep, ritual is one way you can consciously communicate back to your unconscious while you're awake. To the unconscious mind, "real live action" and "conscious intentional ritual" *are the same thing.* By creating a ritual of letting go—for instance, one in which you place an object that symbolizes the clutter of your life on a personal home altar—you can send a powerful message to your subconscious that letting go of clutter is doable and even fun.

Ritual is a great way to anchor your intentions. It helps you to massage and soften and release tough holding patterns and bring to conscious reality the longings of your heart. As Robert A. Johnson says in his book, *Owning Your Own Shadow:*

> You can draw it, sculpt it, write a vivid story about it, dance it, burn something, or bury it—anything that gives expression to that material without doing damage. . . . Remember, a symbolic or ceremonial experience is real and affects one as much as an actual event.

... less and release what no longer
serves and supports you? You could try one of the clearing practices below to
help you... decide... or add a little extra juice to your ritual by creating a s... ...rner of your home or workplace.
Having... ...ur intentions is very powerful.

CLEARING PRACTICES

Choose a... ...or create your own variation.
Notice what it feels like before you do... ...fterward.

...LETTING GO

Detach: Repeat to you... ...ot mine." Whenever you
...emotional weather crea... ...g up suddenly, imagine it
blowing (pe... ...way.

Empty: draw a bath... sh... ...agine the draining water
... ...d beliefs.

Space Clear: ... incen... ...lap, shake a rattle, or ring
... ...or to prepare a space for
something...

Burn: Release behaviors... ...tters, or thoughts written
...with page... Wa... ...

Soften: Release... ...wlike g... ...n an issue or thing by imagining it s... ...ing, unclen... ...ting, and/or sloughing off.

Release: ...letter to s... ...s if you were going to send
... ...gratitude.

...ing go using a small object
that symbolizes your holding pat... ...rns. Place it on a special
... ...sh it Godspeed and, with
your out breath, release it... ...atitude.

CLEARING JOURNAL

After you've had a chance to symbolically clear something, take a moment to
reflect on the experience in your journal.

◊ I was drawn to a ritual blessing and releasing of _____ because _____

◊ Upon completing the ritual, I felt _____

◊ It is safe for me to bless and release _____ because _____

◊ What I'm most ready to let go of now is _____

◊ One thing that I can do every day this week to support my resolve in letting go of this [thing, thought, emotion] is _____

ENOUGH

14

Sometimes, I forget to eat lunch. So, 3:30 arrives, and
I attack an infant-sized hillock of greasy takeout. I inhale it,
scarcely breathing, a condemned man with minutes 'til dawn.
Two minutes after stopping, yes; I feel like I'm going to die. . . .
What happened? How'd I miss when I'd had enough?
—**Merlin Mann, in** *What Matters Now*

Pigging out is not just about consuming food. It can also be trying too hard, overthinking, talking ad nauseam, buying way more than you need or could possibly use, and spending mindless hours glued to the computer or TV set or handheld device.

I can certainly relate to all of the above, especially when it comes to my need for perfection. It's amazing that my head hasn't exploded sometimes from analyzing things to death.

But I have a beautiful antidote for whenever I catch myself bingeing on excess of any kind: three phrases.

Three simple phrases that don't look like much on paper, but have magic powers when you insert them—with awareness—into a daily practice of clearing and mindfulness:

```
┌─────────────────────────────┐
│                             │
│       I am enough           │
│                             │
│      I have enough          │
│                             │
│     There is enough         │
│                             │
└─────────────────────────────┘
```

What does it feel like to say these words out loud?

SOFTENING ATTITUDES

The phrases you've just read are part of a series of four sets of phrases that I use to support any kind of physical, mental, or emotional clutter clearing. I call them Softening Attitudes because they are designed to do just that: soften and release belief patterns that lead to stress and stuckness. Together with the Attitudes of Gratitude (introduced in chapter 12), they help to reduce the stringy buildup of mental chatter and emotional charge. They also serve to anchor your intentions for clearing and letting go.

The phrases are not meant to replace your thoughts, but rather to raise their energetic vibration and promote an ever-growing spaciousness between the thoughts. If you do nothing else to further your quest for a lighter home and a clearer life, I invite you to insert any set of phrases into your awareness.

Your experience of this practice can vary greatly from someone else's. For me, several minutes of attitudinal shifting, two to three times a day or whenever I think of it, makes me feel more grounded and spacious. It relaxes my nervous system. I feel less gummed up, less smoggy, less congested (truly, my nasal passages actually open up!). On days that I miss my practice, I'll notice myself getting crankier, my eyes glazing over, and my reserves becoming more depleted. If I start feeling a growing tightness and inflexibility around my lower back and knees, it's a sign to me to that I've fallen off the wagon.

Nothing beats this cosmic lube job for what it gives me every day with very little effort!

Practice any set of Softening Attitudes two or three times daily with your eyes closed for uninterrupted periods of one to twenty minutes or with your eyes open whenever you think of it, and see what they do for you. Try them for at least six weeks if you want to experience their beneficial effects. You may have to concentrate a bit in the beginning to remember the phrases and their order. After a while, they become second nature—like conscious breathing.

CLEARING PRACTICE

The meditation practice outlined below introduces the first set in the series of Softening Attitudes in this book. This practice is not about repeating the phrase or expecting a certain outcome. It's about clearing the noisy stuff in between what holds the charge.

Clear the charge, and lightness follows.

SIMPLE MEDITATION 1—ENOUGH

1. **Begin** by finding a quiet and comfortable place to sit where you won't be interrupted for at least five to twenty minutes.

2. **Close your eyes** and settle into your chair or cushion, and notice the ambient sounds around you. Breathe. Allow.

3. **Insert** the first phrase of the series, "I am enough," into your consciousness—like a pebble in a still pond—allowing the mind to do whatever it does. You do not need to coordinate the phrase with your breath.

4. **Repeat** the same phrase if you wish, or **move on** to the next phrase, "I have enough," as if you were tossing another pebble.

5. **Move on** to the third phrase when you feel ready: "There is enough."

6. **Take it easy.** If the phrases begin to come through like bullets, notice this and slow it down. This is not about seeing how many "pebbles" you can throw into the water. The idea is to hang out with each phrase in your awareness, one pebble at a time, observing the ripples it creates.

7. **Observe** thoughts and feelings without managing or controlling them in any way. Allow weather to show up in any of its many forms.

8. **Bring yourself back** whenever you feel your mind beginning to wander; take it as a clue to repeat another phrase. Seconds or minutes may pass between each phrase. As the mind grows more still and quiet, you may experience longer stretches between each phrase and thought.

9. **Repeat** the series until one to twenty minutes have passed.

10. **Finish** by taking an easy breath in and out; open your eyes and notice what the world looks like to you now. Do you feel different from how you did before you began?

CLEARING JOURNAL

Use this space and these prompts to reflect on your experience of the first simple meditation.

◊ What I noticed before and after doing this simple practice was _____

◊ I am enough because _____

◊ How I know I have enough is _____

◊ Why I know there is always enough to go around is _____

PRIORITIZE

15

Remembering that you are going to die
is the best way I know to avoid the trap of thinking
you have something to lose. You are already
naked. There is no reason not to follow your heart.
—Steve Jobs

Among the many wonderful emails I have received from students after a workshop or retreat, there is one that really stood out for me. I love it not just because it showcases the exquisite expressions of clutter and clearing, but because it landed in my inbox at the precise moment that I needed it for my revision of this book. In her message below, participant and fellow writer Betsy Bowen shares her reflections on how things are going for her since the course ended:

> I have also been having some interesting reactions, but more along the lines of realizing how much of reality is more muddled fantasy. It's apparent when I realize how deeply attached I am to articles of clothing that will never, ever fit again and don't match my life.
>
> In fact, last night, I saw an HBO documentary called "Remembering Triangle," about the Triangle Shirt Waist fire of 1911, wherein 138 underpaid and overworked women died in 18 minutes—90 of them jumping from 9th floor windows to escape flames. The

73

documentarian interviewed family members who told stories of relatives they had lost in the fire.

One of the stories involved a young man, engaged to be married, who made it out of the building but ran back inside when he realized he had left his grandfather's gold pocket watch. His body was so charred, his fiancée was unable to identify it, until they found the pocket watch in his clothes. When they opened it, her photograph was inside. They said she had to be carried out of the morgue.

I saw that and started thinking, "So what's more important to me—a pair of gray wool flannel Amalfi slacks, several sizes too small, or my life right now?" Although I probably wouldn't run into a fire to save them, I certainly give space and precious energy to their preservation. They're like a shrine to a former self, when being thin and glamorous and wearing eye-catching clothes was everything. People didn't even like me, and I was competitive and miserable. So what the hell? Why hang on to a character flaw?

Amen, sister!

WEIGHTY REGRETS

So you're on your deathbed. You've lived a long and vibrant life. You have your family around you. You're ready to cross over, feeling very content and complete—on to the next adventure waiting for you on the other side. What would you like to say as your parting words to your friends, family, world?

This question was inspired by a post I read called "Regrets of the Dying" by Bronnie Ware, a nurse who spent years with dying people.

According to Ware, in this excerpt from her blog, these are the top five regrets that people have on their deathbed:

1. I wish I'd had the courage to live a life true to myself, not the life others expected of me.

2. I wish I didn't work so hard.

3. I wish I'd had the courage to express my feelings.

4. I wish I had stayed in touch with my friends.

5. I wish that I had let myself be happier.

There is still time for most of us to make some changes, time to live the life that has been waiting for us all along, time to release any regrets that keep us stuck in the past, time to discover and enjoy a little heaven on earth before it's time to actually go there.

As one who plans to go the distance in this lifetime, I hope that my parting words will be something along the lines of: *"Wow. That was one hell of a ride."*

CLEARING PRACTICE
PRIORITIZING

If this were the last day or week of your life, what would you let go of? What would you make room to do that you don't usually make time for? Who would you call or talk to?

It doesn't have to be some fancy "bucket list" of greatest hits, either. You could choose to focus on feeling *really good*—just for today. Your list could be as simple as this:

◊ Let all calls go to voice mail.

◊ Have a cup of tea, really good tea, and sip it.

◊ Spend a (guilt-free) day wearing pajamas and watching some favorite TV reruns.

CLEARING JOURNAL

Use this time and the prompts below to get in touch with what really matters to you.

◊ I am on the planet because _____

◊ When I'm on my deathbed, I want to be saying _____

◊ I am worthy of realizing my deepest dreams and desires because _____

◊ I trust Divine Intelligence to support me in realizing what I came here to do and be because _____

◊ I know that things beyond my control are "already handled" because _____

16 "RE"-MIND

Before you speak, ask yourself: Is it necessary?
Is it true? Is it kind? Will it improve on the silence?
—Shirdi Sai Baba

Very few of us humans can look at an image of a battle, a politician, a chocolate bar, a starving child, a hurricane, or a gorgeous movie star—as a few examples—and not have an opinion about it. Our conditioning and body chemistry have us programmed to judge the image as being good or bad, positive or negative, right or wrong, better or worse. In fact, if we really paid attention, most of our thoughts are polarized or polarizing in one way or another.

The famine in Africa—bad; ninth-grade science teacher—bad (if he didn't have the comb-over, he might be tolerable); the rain—good for the gardener/bad for the wedding . . . Whatever the assessment, it simply becomes another filter and lens through which we view, create, and distort our reality. To the degree that we are not completely lost in our own dramas and can bring awareness to our moment-to-moment experiences, we can choose differently.

Here's the rub: If the same beliefs have been spinning around for an entire lifetime, it might take a while and lots of gentle "minding" to soften their grip.

Which is why we're back to revisiting the topic of mental clutter. Clearing persisting patterns can look a lot like the movie *Groundhog Day,* in which Bill Murray's character wakes up each morning to an exact replica of the day he had before—again and again—until he "gets" the lesson to be a kinder person.

No matter how colorful they are, stories have nothing to do with what is going on in present time. So what's going through your mind right this second?

◊ Do you have thirty-five things spinning around in your head at the same time?

◊ Are you skimming this page as quickly as possible so that you can get on to the next thing on your to-do list?

◊ Are you thinking, *Didn't we cover this already in part 1?*

◊ Are you wondering if you're going to learn something practical, more concrete?

◊ Are you attentive? Bored? Engaged? Curious? Overwhelmed? Stimulated?

◊ How's your breathing? Is it shallow; is it full?

Yes, it does seem like an echo from the previous part on awareness, the same quality of noisy chatter, the same invitation to tune in, the same practice of bringing mindfulness to the situation.

But as in *Groundhog Day,* the big difference here is that it's a new minute, a new opportunity to cultivate awareness, a new opportunity to come back into balance.

Bringing the light of awareness to *any* thought—without doing anything to fix, change, manage, or medicate it—reduces internal noise and chatter, calms the mind, and e-x-p-a-n-d-s the quiet space around the thoughts.

One minute at a time.

CLEARING PRACTICE
MINDING AND MINING

Close your eyes. Take a nice, easy breath in, then a slow, emptying breath out. Breathe out all thought and tension. Breathe in pure awareness and possibility. Notice and *allow* how you are feeling at this moment—without judging it as good or bad or taking it personally.

Reflect on how the clearing journey is going for you so far.

CLEARING JOURNAL

As we come to the conclusion of part 2, this is as good a time as any to stop and reflect on how things might be shifting for you in general.

◊ Some of the ways that I feel lighter since I started reading this book are _____

◊ My biggest challenge with clearing the clutter in my life has been _____

◊ I have been pleasantly surprised by my experience of _____

◊ Ways that have helped me navigate the bumpy weather when it arises have been _____

◊ My biggest take-away so far has been _____

INTENTION

Where the mind goes, energy flows.

Intention gives the clearing vehicle its direction.

Our job is to feel what we truly desire and let go of attachment to the outcome.

Sending out signals of what we resist or do not desire will attract these also.

"Acting as if" helps us to anchor our deepest yearnings.

Ritual is a way we can communicate with our unconscious mind.

Reframing our beliefs is like creating new software; it helps to tame the monkey mind.

Expressing gratitude is clearing.

Practicing the Softening Attitudes will raise our energy level, reduce stress, and support new habits of clearing.

Having no regrets is clearing.

PART III

ACTION
GO SLOW TO GO FAST

Nature does not hurry, yet everything is accomplished.
—Lao Tzu

17 CLEARING WITH ACTION

When you are rushed, vital connections are lost.
—**Anonymous**

LESS IS MORE

It was June 1985 when the twenty-one-year-old mountaineer Joe Simpson and his climbing partner, twenty-five-year-old Simon Yates, became the first ever to successfully ascend the twenty-one-thousand-foot Siula Grande west face in the Peruvian Andes. The feat itself, though incredible, is nothing compared to what ensued for these two men as they made their final, grueling descent.

If it weren't bad enough for Joe Simpson to have broken a leg in three places, he then plunged down a crevasse in the middle of the night to the horror of his climbing partner and miraculously negotiated a terrifying exit down a gigantic glacier with a limited length of rope. But what is beyond imagining is the remarkable journey of a man dragging his broken body for several days, alone, back to base camp with only one good leg and nothing to eat or drink.

Assuming the worst, and having no means to find his friend without killing himself, the helpless and grieving Yates had no other recourse but to do the only thing he could: leave his partner behind.

What got Simpson through his ordeal, he says, was setting the most precise goals. In his film *Touching the Void,* he describes how his mind, using simple dispassionate commands, directed him to advance: *Go from here to the edge of that rock in twenty minutes. . . . Get from here to the edge of that crevasse in fifteen minutes.* He would set the timer on his watch and, like a rag doll flopping on its belly, drag himself across the inhospitable maze of high-altitude glaciers and boulders to his next stop. It would take him hours to cover a few hundred feet. He says that if he had considered the sheer enormity of the task to survive, he could never have done it. Nearly delirious—having lost one third of his total body weight—he managed in the end to meet up with his incredulous partner and lived to tell the story.

If Joe Simpson had not been able to reduce his task to smaller, manageable steps that his mind could handle, he would not have survived. Setting doable tasks and sticking with them, no matter how small they seem in the bigger scheme, is the name of the game in clearing, too.

CLEARING WITH ACTION

If intention is what steers the clearing vehicle, action is what gives it gas. You can have all the intention in the world, but if you don't back it up with some level of modest movement, you won't get very far. As Will Rogers once said, "Even if you're on the right track, you'll get run over if you just sit there."

It is important to remember that action, as it relates to clearing in this book, is not simply about "doing" something to rid the home of excess. Clearing with action is not necessarily a means to an end, like taking out the trash or taking stuff to the Goodwill or having a yard sale. As we have learned and will continue to explore, there is a powerful action in *repetition*, in *practice*, in *mindfulness*, in *surrender*. The simple practices of putting away, rounding up, and addressing tolerations—those household annoyances and unfinished projects that have been sitting around for so long, you don't even notice them anymore—may not constitute "clearing," per se, but they are terrific action steps that are sure to get the energy moving in your home and life.

For those of you who find the idea of taking baby steps unsatisfying or even excruciating, you may be glad to know that there is an important reason for this. It's called the human brain. In this part, you will learn that you cannot possibly create a clearing habit that is both sustaining and sustainable without taking into account the role of our instinctive fight-or-flight response to stress. You will see how, by keeping your focus on "small" and by setting your mind on "doable," you *can* make progress at anything you desire.

Like a butterfly's wings in one part of the world creating massive weather changes in another, so too can baby steps lead to a sea change in your life; a clearing movement of global proportions!

CHOOSE EASE 18

When you feel overwhelmed, you're trying too hard.
—**Thich Nhat Hanh**

Ease.

For such a little word, it lingers and expands if you say it out loud. With very little effort, it works magic on your nervous system.

So why is this little word so *not* easy to cultivate sometimes? What could possibly get in the way?

That would be our old pal monkey mind and his entourage of fearful thoughts and the corresponding release of stress hormones that keep us in a permanent state of alert.

Whenever you're feeling overwhelmed (stuck in a rut, fearful, pissed-off, resistant, recalcitrant . . .), you can bet that a switch just went off in the ancient part of your brain triggering a thing called the fight-or-flight response.

This survival mechanism is generated by the amygdala, which plays a key role in processing our emotions in the most primitive part of our brains. It is our built-in secret-service agent, if you will. It springs into action the moment it senses danger (*read:* you've stepped out of your comfort zone, gotten in over your head, taken on more than you can chew . . . in *real* danger).

It's a good thing to have when a lion is charging at you, or your kid is about to step into traffic, or a car swerves into your lane. But it's not all that helpful when the fight-or-flight response kicks in unexpectedly while you're clearing out an attic full of letters that your old boyfriend wrote you in high school or watching your only child go off to college or preparing to talk to a roomful of expectant students.

So how do you disconnect the thing so that the alarm bells aren't going off at all hours?

You can't. It's hard-wired.

You can, however, *make friends with it* when you

◊ bring awareness to how you feel, especially before your circuits get fried.

◊ feel your feelings without taking them personally.

◊ reduce your area of focus to one thing or activity.

◊ adopt a daily practice of self-care that feels good and nourishes you instead.

◊ repeat the phrase "I choose ease" whenever you think of it.

◊ practice the simple meditation outlined in the clearing practice below.

Adopting any one or all of these will help keep your monkey mind off his high horse.

FIGHT OR FLIGHT

If scientific concepts and big unpronounceable words make your head spin like they do mine sometimes, you'll love the wonderful little book that helped me understand what exactly happens biochemically when we get lost in overwhelm La-la Land.

The book is called *One Small Step Can Change Your Life*, and was written by psychologist Dr. Robert Maurer. In it, he talks about the role of the amygdala—the three-million-year-old almond-sized part of our brain that governs the fight-or-flight response. He explains why humans get overwhelmed and makes a compelling case for doing what feels so counterintuitive for most of us: going slow and simplifying.

It is no secret that stepping out of our comfort zone to clear all manner of attachments can, and will, set off alarm bells from time to time. The more stuck, attached, and unconscious we are, the bigger the potential for slipping and falling into the rabbit hole of fear I write about in chapter 5.

According to Maurer, however, there *is* a simple way to bypass our internal wiring; a way to trick the amygdala into thinking that everything is cool and right with the world.

Maurer suggests taking the tiniest, sometimes even the most "embarrassingly trivial" steps in the beginning. For the person who wants to cut out caffeine, for example, he might suggest they take one less sip each day. For those who cannot bring themselves to floss their teeth, he suggests flossing just one tooth a day. Overspending? He recommends taking one thing out of the shopping cart before heading to the cash register. According to Maurer, this principle applies to any change, "whether the goal is ending a nail-biting habit or learning to say no."

Sounds outrageous perhaps, but if there is a simple task or behavior change you wish to bring into your life that has so far eluded you, this slow-drip approach makes sense. It is user-friendly, and, more importantly, it works.

It works because, as the saying goes, "neurons that fire together wire together." Every time you repeat a task, your brain is creating new wiring, a new infrastructure to support a clear(er) *way of life*. As Maurer puts it:

> As your small steps continue and your cortex starts working, the brain begins to create "software" for your desired change, actually laying down new nerve pathways and building new habits.

Applying small efforts consistently over time is the real game changer in clutter clearing; the payoff is enormous.

You will find in the long run that snipping off a dead leaf from the plant or fluffing up the pillows or sweeping the kitchen floor—with awareness *every day*—will create more lasting benefits than if you go on an unconscious binge of clearing the nightmare in your basement. Clearing one small thing at a time with intention is all it takes to soften resistance, get the energy moving, and build the sense of safety needed to clear an entire household.

Add gratitude to the mix, and you've created a potent formula for lasting change!

CLEARING PRACTICE
CHOOSING EASE

The practice of choosing ease is really quite simple (even with the monkey mind horning in from time to time). Our old habits and limiting thoughts keep us stuck believing that things have to be complicated, hard, and *not easy*.

Try it now: repeat the phrase "I choose ease" and notice how you feel. Breathe it in and "receive" the phrase like a sponge soaking up water.

Insert the phrase "I choose ease" into your daily routine or a difficult situation, and you may notice the feeling of "expanding into" other wonderful sensations.

Repeat the phrase at least once today or as often as you can remember, and take a few moments at the end of the day to reflect on your experience in your journal. [*Psst,* don't be discouraged if it takes a while to get this. I've found that repeating these three little words eludes even my most advanced students.]

You can take your practice a step further and adopt the second set of Softening Attitudes as a daily meditation detailed below.

The second set of phrases is:

I choose ease

I choose peace

I choose joy

SIMPLE MEDITATION 2—EASE

1. **Begin** by finding a quiet and comfortable place to sit where you won't be interrupted for at least five minutes.

2. **Close** your eyes and settle into your chair or cushion, and notice the ambient sounds around you. Breathe. Allow.

3. **Insert** the first phrase of the series, "I choose ease." Drop it into your consciousness—like a pebble in a still pond—allowing the mind to do whatever it does. You do not need to coordinate the phrase with your breath.

4. **Repeat** the same phrase if you wish, or move on the next phrase, "I choose peace," as if you were tossing another pebble.

5. **Move on** when you're ready to the third phrase, "I choose joy."

6. **Observe** thoughts and feelings without managing or controlling them in any way. Allow weather to show up in any of its many forms. As the mind grows more still and quiet, you may experience longer stretches between each phrase and thought.

7. When you feel complete, **finish** by wiggling your fingers and your toes; open your eyes and notice how you feel. Notice what the world looks like to you now. Do you feel different from how you did before you began?

CLEARING JOURNAL

Take a moment to reflect on the simple practice of choosing ease.

◊ When I repeat the phrase "I choose ease" and fully receive it (like a sponge soaking up water), I feel _____

◊ It is safe for me to choose ease because _____

◊ What I noticed in my body and mind before the meditation, and after, was _____

◊ What I'm noticing in the world "out there" when I cultivate greater ease, peace, and joy "in here" (in my mind) is _____

19   START WHERE YOU ARE

Start where you are. Use what you have. Do what you can.

—Arthur Ashe

POP QUIZ (SPACIOUS STYLE)

Take one minute to answer the following questions. A simple yes or no will do.

◊ Is there something in your purse or wallet that doesn't need to be there?

◊ Is there something on the floor (that doesn't need to be there)?

◊ Do you have stuff in the fridge or freezer that is over six months old?

◊ Do you have an unfinished project that you've held on to for over a year?

◊ Is there something you did today that felt like a "should"?

◊ Are you aggravated by someone in your life? A family member, co-worker, or housemate?

◊ Are you feeling like life is just passing you by, and you have nothing to show for it?

◊ Are these questions pissing you off?

◊ Are you feeling even the slightest hint of overwhelm?

◊ Are you feeling the impulse to "fix" the problem right away?

◊ Are you able to accept things just as they are?

◊ Are you aware of your breathing?

Time's up.

Whatever your response, if you brought awareness to any one of these questions by feeling whatever you were feeling or allowing your cage to be rattled the tiniest little bit, *you passed!* Congratulations.

CLEARING IS NOT LINEAR

In all my years doing this work, it all boils down to this:

◊ Clearing is an opportunity to bring compassionate awareness to the places in your home and life that are out of balance.

◊ Clearing is a journey that doesn't always add up, make sense, or go in a straight line.

◊ Clearing is a daily practice that starts where you are.

Whatever your particular issue is today, if you can embrace the moment and allow the simplicity of Arthur Ashe's message to cut you some slack (and cut to the chase), *you are clearing.*

(No matter what the monkey mind has to say about it.)

REDUCE AND REPEAT (R&R)

For those of you who have battled a lifetime of physical, mental, and/or emotional clutter and find the stress hormones coursing through your body at the mere sight of your piles, your email inbox, or your to-do list, I offer you my gentler "reduce and repeat" approach to clearing. It is designed to bypass the fight-or-flight response to give your clearing efforts some traction that can lead to lasting change. Remember that baby steps and repetition are the keys to creating new pathways in the brain.

Here's how it works: Anytime you feel challenged and overwhelmed in your effort to cultivate a clear home and spacious life, take it as a sign to *reduce* the task, time spent, and/or clearing perimeter to a more manageable size, and *repeat* the task until it is complete. The R&R approach to clearing the refrigerator, for example, could be to clean, clear, or consolidate one item, pile, or area. You could start with the leftovers, move on to the condiments, and end with the frozen food. If it takes you three days or three weeks, that's what it takes.

Be sure to apply the "rule of one" to your practice: take any task and reduce your area of focus to *one* thing, one pile, or one space, and clear (or just move) it once a day, for one week. For some of you, this may be the tiniest of steps: just opening one drawer and peeking inside it, once a day, for one week, until you have the courage and energy to actually take out one piece of paper or candy wrapper or dull pencil nub. The point here is not volume but the consistency.

If physical clutter is not your thing and clearing it doesn't stir the fight-or-flight response in the least, there is something here for you, too. Perhaps you have a behavior or issue that you would like to change in your life. Perhaps you're a compulsive worrier; or a telephone, tabloid, or bad news junkie; or someone who is chronically late for appointments. The R&R approach can address these issues, too.

If you're a bit of a control freak, like me, who suffers from the need to call the shots, make things perfect, and eliminate all margins for error, the "rule of one" can be very useful. Maybe you feel totally stale and uncreative. Maybe you're too serious and don't play enough or laugh enough or have enough fun. Maybe you just can't bring yourself to smile at your co-worker or the cute guy who rides your bus every day. The R&R approach is perfect for any number of behaviors that gum us up.

Be creative. Find some way to dial it down by reducing, in small increments, the number of times you repeat an undesirable action or, conversely, increasing a desired action by one repetition at a time. Remember to go at a rate that is not threatening and does not kick in the body's fight-or-flight response.

Decrease by telling one less piece of gossip a day. Decrease by reading one less bad news story in the paper each morning. Increase a desired action with one extra smile or allowing one mistake a day. You can make adjustments along the way to the degree that you feel more safe and are moved to do so. Key again: consistency.

[*Psst,* don't forget to stop and feel. These are wonderful opportunities to become more aware of the places you hold on.]

CLEARING PRACTICE
TUNING IN TO WHERE YOU ARE

In your journal, write down any of the questions from the list at the beginning of this chapter that elicited a reaction, and add to it any other issues that hold an emotional charge for you.

When you're finished, *slowly* scroll down your list, stopping and noting the issues that continue to elicit a twitch, an eyebrow rise, shallow breathing, a nervous laugh, sweaty palms, a tightening in the jaw or fist, fatigue—any sensation that points to a button getting pressed.

Notice your impulse to "do something," fix, and/or manage your discomfort.

Notice your breathing. (Is it shallow? Is it relaxed?)

CLEARING JOURNAL

Use your clearing journal to reflect on the areas in your home and life that overwhelm you. Add your own variations to more effectively release your personal emotional charge.

◊ The issues in my life to which I would like to bring awareness are _____

◊ Tuning in to sensations and my own emotional weather while doing this clearing practice brings up feelings of _____

◊ I can more readily address waves of self-judgment, blame, and other overwhelming feelings when they arise because _____

◊ One issue that I can address right now [sometime today] is

_____

◊ Right this minute, I'm feeling [*psst,* this is a new minute; note if you're feeling the same or different from the last time you checked] _____

20   MOVE SOMETHING

At the heart of it, mastery is practice.
Mastery is staying on the path.
—**George Leonard**

I often hear stories from my clients and students that the biggest clutter-clearing challenge is not the clearing part, *per se*. Their biggest problem is getting their partner, kids, family members, or even neighbors to clear up their own !?/@#*& mess!

No question, a daily dose of tripping over sneakers, newspapers, hampers of unfolded laundry, piles of this and that is enough to make anyone feel defeated from the get-go. We can lead a horse to the proverbial clearing well, but in the end, we can't force it to do a thing with it. To the degree that we get plugged in, for better or worse, their clutter becomes our clutter. There is no separation.

The good news is that as you embark on your *own* clearing journey, you create significant energetic openings. Though the effects might not be immediately obvious, the Law of Attraction ensures that these openings can and will produce a powerful ripple effect that will attract more possibilities for clearing.

When you harp on your beloved family members for being slobs, you create a less-desirable ripple effect of divisiveness and polarization that feeds old patterns and yields more stubborn defensiveness.

When have pestering and haranguing ever delivered the goods?

Clearing begets more clearing. Moving energy creates more energy. What, how much, and when is irrelevant. The point is, the less attached you can be to the outcome of your efforts, the more spaciousness you create on every level.

So here's my advice:

◊ Focus on clearing your own "mess."

◊ Let go of attachment to clearing other people's messes.

◊ Allow the ripple effect to work its magic.

MOVING ENERGY

No one would argue that we live in a culture that possesses many things, and the transfer of those things is a way of life for us. Why not use it to our advantage?

Here's what I know about possessions and moving them around:

◊ Moving things from one place to another—clothes to drawer, grocery bag to car, dishes to dishwasher, magazines to reading pile, button that needs sewing to to-do pile, bills to desk drawer (or wherever they go in your house), dirty clothes to hamper, attic treasures to Goodwill—*moves energy.*

◊ Moving energy releases stuck energy.

◊ Sometimes the release of stuck energy doesn't feel very good (especially if the thing has been sitting around for a while).

◊ Adding awareness to any task of moving is called "clearing."

CLEARING PRACTICE

Try this simple, one-minute clearing practice.

ONE-MINUTE CLEARING

1. **Stop.** Put this book down, or close your computer, and take a good look around you. See if there is something out of place that could be put back in its usual home. (If it doesn't have a home, consider giving it one.)

2. **Notice** what it feels like to see it out of place.

3. Notice what it feels like to put it away in its regular or new home.

4. Notice if this simple practice of putting away brings up some resistance.

5. Notice what is going through your mind.

6. Notice your breathing.

7. That's it. **Time's up.**

CLEARING JOURNAL

After completing the clearing practice, take a moment to reflect on the experience using these statements.

◊ What I noticed and felt when I looked up from what I was doing was _____

◊ What I'm noticing (and feeling) about placing my focus on just one thing, one task, for one minute is _____

◊ It is easy to put things away because _____

◊ One simple thing I can do to "move energy" today [every day this week] is _____

PLACE

21

There are hundreds of ways to kneel and kiss the ground.

—Rumi

Can you remember the last time you consciously placed an object in its designated home? Yes, *placed.* As opposed to tossed, squeezed, jammed, shoved, crammed, bent, threw, wadded, scrunched.

"Place" as in:

◊ Lay grocery bags in the trunk of your car in such a way that they don't fall over and smash the eggs.

◊ Take a few extra seconds to consciously put the food in the refrigerator so that you can see and find everything later.

◊ Fold a garment with appreciation for its texture, detailing, color, and the important role it plays in your life.

◊ Match shoes with mates.

◊ Sort the mail into piles as soon it comes in the door: letters, bills, magazines, catalogues, recycling.

◊ Park the car so that it's easy to get in and out of and less likely to be rammed into by another car.

◊ Prominently display a gorgeous bouquet of flowers where you can see them every time you walk by.

◊ Move the chairs back under the table when not in use.

Inserting love and awareness into any ordinary task raises its positive vibration—and yours.

PLACEMENT HAS ITS PLACE

If everything is energy, then it's fair to say that the simple act of moving things around will release stagnant energy—no matter what it is. Rounding up a pile on your desk or putting the reading glasses back in their home or simply moving some clutter from one corner to another gets the energy moving! It is a great way to gather up all the loose ends *(strings)* of the day. What's more, these practices have the added benefit of creating new neural pathways in the brain. They relax the central nervous system and produce feelings of calm and well-being.

Years ago, when I was a teenager, I spent a summer as a Montessori school teacher's assistant for three- to five-year olds. Even back then, I was astonished by the level of harmony and peacefulness that prevailed in the classroom. For Maria Montessori, the idea of placement was integral to her philosophy and continues to be a principal teaching tool for developing gross and fine motor skills. Kids as young as two and a half years of age learn to respect their space and each other at a very deep level.

In every Montessori classroom, there are cubbies and containers to house every object that a child uses. Things are grouped by function and size: larger blocks together, medium blocks together, and so on. Children can play with anything they like, provided they put it back where they found it before moving on to the next toy, game, or activity. Teachers help kids instill these habits by taking their hands and physically guiding them to the appropriate cubby or container, every time, until they master the task.

For the Japanese, housing things and putting them away is an essential way of life, not only for its practical benefits but also as a high form of artistic expression. The homes I visited when I was in Japan years ago felt to me like temples; they embodied a simple elegance that was immediately restful and inviting. I was moved by the conscious placement of things: a window framing the garden just so to draw the eye through the interior space in a very restful way; shoes and slippers lined up neatly in the foyer for easy access; futon beds and linens stored during the day behind beautiful *soji* screens to allow a space to serve many uses. The Japanese have much less living space in actual square footage than we do in this country, and still they manage to create a level of spaciousness that far exceeds our own.

The Shaker tradition doesn't hide its useful things behind screens like the Japanese. The chairs, the broom, the tools of daily living—which are beautiful in their own right—are hung right up on the wall in plain view. I can't imagine any American household suspending their coffee pot or blender, but the idea of having one useful thing that is easy to reach and lovely to look at, instead of dozens of specialty things cluttering the countertops, is very appealing.

Imagine what life would be like if you had designated places for all of your things and learned to put things away consistently: putting the receipts away after paying the bills, putting make-up in the basket after using it, putting dirty clothes in the hamper. It takes, what? One second to toss the shirt in the basket?

So here's what to do:

1. **Find a home** for everything, even if you still cannot bring yourself to put it away immediately as the Montessori kids do. Just knowing that something has its own dedicated space helps to quiet some of the chaos. It also feels good when you can "put things to bed," so to speak. Get yourself a lot of beautiful containers or storage baskets and label them if you have to. This will make your things easy to find later on. If you need help getting started, hire a personal organizer. They are magicians when it comes to optimizing space and creating order out of chaos.

2. **Create breathing room** for your things, if possible. It feels great to put things away into drawers or closets when there is still space left in them. As a squirrel hoarder who used to jam things in so tightly that the closet hinges nearly broke off, this point still feels radical to me. The mere thought of having spaces that remain empty is a huge stretch, and when I am able to pull it off, it feels almost decadent.

3. **Sort things by kind.** Place your dishes together with other dishes. Keep all photos together in one place. Dry goods in bulk together. Art projects together. Liquid items together. All coffee supplies together. Socks together in the drawer. Winter clothes together. Fishing equipment. Skis, boots, poles, helmets. Summer clothes together. Big things together, small together. Things you like looking at up front; less pretty things you need in back. You get the idea.

CLEARING PRACTICE

The practice is to "place" a thing or a thought—with awareness.

MINDFUL PLACEMENT

◊ **Things:** If it's a misplaced object, restore it to its permanent home. For the best effect, choose something that is a bit of a stretch and routinely out of place, like the car keys, reading glasses, the remote control to your television, clean dishes in the cabinet, toothpaste cap on the tube, and so on.

◊ **Thoughts:** If it is a thought that doesn't lift and support you, "re-place" it with a new thought. Insert the new thought into your awareness—like dropping a pebble into a still pond—and watch the ripple effect it creates.

◊ **Other:** If you cannot think of anything at all to work with, spend a minute savoring the moment. Feel what it feels like to have no agenda.

CLEARING JOURNAL

Take a moment to complete and reflect on the following.

◊ It feels really good to consciously place things where they belong because _____

◊ Seeing things out of place makes me feel _____

◊ Some things that still need a home are _____

◊ Some of the thoughts that most nourish me are _____

◊ This practice is showing me that I can more easily release _____

PUT AWAY EVERY DAY

22

> How we hold the simplest of our tasks
> speaks loudly about how we hold life itself.
> —**Gunilla Norris**, *Being Home*

NO HOME, NO HAVE

I have a client who realized that what she needed was easy access to her purse every day, but because it had no "home," she kept tripping over it on her way out the front door. Leaving the house was like navigating a slalom course of purses, keys, coats, and shoes. She admitted that it was an awful way to start the day. This one issue, however, forced her to consider the usefulness of the bookcase that took up prime real estate in the front entrance of her house—smack dab where her purse and car keys would logically go. Moving her beloved books to another, more sensible location—such as the study or living area—would require that she displace (or clear) something else to make room for the bookcase.

Finding a home for her one little purse started a musical-chair movement of clearing that affected the entire house.

I once saw this staggering statistic in *Newsweek:* "It takes the average American fifty-five minutes every day—[adding up to] roughly twelve weeks a year—looking for things they know they own but can't find." Though I've thought that this outdated factoid (which always seemed a bit exaggerated) could not possibly relate to me, I had to smile when I found myself tearing my entire office apart looking for this very quotation to make my point! I can't say that it took me fifty-five minutes to locate it, but, if I added the time it took me to look for the sales receipt I needed to return a set of curtain rods plus find the phone number for a subscription I wanted to cancel, I suppose you could say I'm getting up there.

These are the obvious reasons for giving every thing a home, of course. Having a place for everything helps you keep things in order and find them again. It helps us get to the car in the morning without tripping over shoes, backpacks, or purses. Giving things a home also helps us know when we have too much stuff. Finding zero space in the bookcase to jam another paperback or zero hangers for the new outfit we just bought on sale, for example, gives us instant feedback that something has to give or something has to go. Housing things properly holds us accountable and keeps us honest.

But there is more going on here than the obvious. If you consider the concept of "participatory relationship," there is something organic, alive, and vital that connects us to our homes and our things. Giving an object that you use and love a dedicated space recognizes its purpose and honors its value.

Papers, bottles, sticky candy wrappers strewn in the back seat of the car, for example, or store catalogues scattered helter-skelter or leftovers molding on the kitchen counter, represent way more than "poor slob" or hopeless human behaviors. To me they reflect a level of unconsciousness; a deep disconnect from our environment and our world at large. If you wonder how this can be so, just stop for a moment and imagine your home and your possessions as members of your family.

What does it feel like—physically and emotionally—to neglect or disrespect your home and your things?

So here's my tough-love position on this issue: No matter how precious or valuable or critical your things may be to your personal survival, self-concept, health, or well-being, unless you have a permanent and dedicated place to put them, they are . . . *clutter!*

This means, simply: no home, no have.

CLEARING PRACTICE

Jump-starting, cultivating, or maintaining a daily clearing practice requires motivation and a certain degree of locomotion. Here are three ways to create momentum when time and energy are in short supply. They are also terrific ways to promote mindfulness and create new pathways in your home, life, and brain!

Choose one and go for it!

THREE WAYS TO PUT AWAY EVERY DAY

1. **Put away one thing:** Take a look at the room you're sitting in. If it's your home or workplace, do a quick scan and see if there is one thing here that you are not using right now that is not in its designated home. Now—here's the hard part (hee-hee)—get up and put it where it belongs! If it doesn't have a home, consider the question *why* and the possibility that it, or something else, will have to go. After you have relocated the object, ask yourself these questions: How hard was that, really? What does it feel like to consciously place this thing in its proper place every time? How does the room feel now?

2. **Put away the same thing in the same place:** This practice involves putting away the *same* thing every day. First, choose one thing that you can commit to putting away every day for one week. Choose something that is a stretch but will not elicit stress hormones. Second, find a home for it where it will stay for at least a week. Third, put it away *every day.* After a week of this, notice how it feels. Notice how hard it was. Notice if it has stirred any resistance. Notice if this simple exercise promoted an ease of putting away other things you hadn't planned on addressing. Here are some examples of things you can put away every day:

   • car keys, reading glasses, remote control, cell phone

   • coats, clothing, shoes

   • dirty clothes in the hamper

- clean clothes in the closet or drawer
- book on the nightstand instead of the floor

Even the *smallest* actions of putting away every day can make a difference in changing the energy in your life. For example:

- Turn out lights that are not in use.
- Turn off the TV or radio.
- Put the toilet seat down.
- Close drawers until you hear the "click."
- Push chairs in after eating or working at the desk.
- Sharpen the pencils.
- Make the bed.
- Close or open the curtains/shades.
- Push the toothpaste in the tube up and put the cap on.

3. **Round it up in sixty seconds:**

- **Pick a space,** any space, in your home or office. At the end of the day, take sixty seconds to put everything away.

- **Pick it up.** If it's the family room, pick up the newspapers and place in the recycling bin or the "to read" basket, stack the magazines on the coffee table, return dirty dishes to the kitchen, place toys in the toy box, fluff up the pillows and thump the sofa cushions, rewind the videotape, eject the DVD, close the TV cabinet, shut the curtains or blinds, turn the light switch off.

- **Be mindful.** This does *not* mean reading the article in the paper that immediately catches your eye. It does not mean taking the dog out for a quick walk. This does not mean washing the dishes or making a phone call. This does not mean ranting at family members who left a huge pile of dirty dishes. This task is simply to pick up the room to the best of your ability in less than one minute.

- **Have fun.** Make it quick and fun. Get the kids, partners, housemates, or co-workers to help. Challenge people to see how many things they can put away in sixty seconds by counting them out and declare a winner for the day.

- **Set a timer.** Time yourself the first time you do this if you think it takes too long. Can you do this in less than sixty seconds?

- **Notice.** How does it feel to return to this space the next morning?

[*Psst,* remember, if it's too much to do a whole room, *reduce* the roundup perimeter to smaller areas or piles in your home. If it's too easy to do one room, *expand* the roundup perimeter to include other piles or spaces in your home.]

CLEARING JOURNAL

Based on your experience of dialing it down, take a moment to complete and consider the following.

◊ Some of the tasks that typically elude me are [*psst,* be aware of the critical mind attempting to pipe in by noticing any contracting sensations that may arise] _____

◊ It feels really good to tend to my home because _____

◊ Bringing a quality of mindfulness to ordinary housekeeping tasks feels _____

◊ One simple task I can reasonably accomplish right now [every day this week] is _____

23 SORT

Not hammer-strokes, but dance of the water,
sings the pebbles into perfection.
—Rabindranath Tagore

There is no better way to get the energy moving fast (and come face to face with your "holding on" patterns) than to take a regular dip into that thing you carry around everywhere you go: your purse or wallet. This is, in fact, what I invite workshop participants to do.

Ten minutes into my presentation, I'll have everyone grab their bags, purses, wallets, or whatever carrier they brought with them and dump the entire contents on a table or the floor.

The room begins to look like Christmas morning or Hanukkah *after* the presents have been unwrapped, and the kids have scampered off to play with their treasures. The colorful reveals have been known to include:

◊ 8 lipsticks (in one purse)

◊ 14–20 pens

◊ a paper bag full of store receipts

◊ miscellaneous movie stubs, parking tickets, gum wrappers

◊ hair-care products

◊ multiple bottles of sunscreen in various stages of use

◊ gigantic key rings (the size of a prison guard's) jangling with numerous and often unidentifiable keys in multiple shapes and sizes

Add to the experience a soundtrack of groans and *Oh my God, that's where that went* exclamations, and you get the picture.

Once it's all out on the table or floor, I invite participants to group the contents into four piles: **stay, go, throw, don't know.** In less than ten minutes, everyone has not only cleared a mountain of stuff they didn't even know they had but discovered clutter clearing's secret weapon: humor.

After that, it's time to sort, keep it simple, and be ruthless.

ACID TESTS FOR CLEARING AND ACQUIRING

When you find yourself not knowing whether something is clutter or not or find yourself in a shop swooning over yet another jacket just like the twenty others you have at home, you can drop into your intuitive self and apply the Acid Test for Clearing, described here, or the Acid Test for Acquiring, which follows.

ACID TEST FOR CLEARING

1. Do I absolutely love it?

2. Do I genuinely need it?

3. Does it have a permanent home?

Here's what they mean:

Do I Absolutely Love It?

◊ Does this lift my spirits?

◊ Does this make my heart sing?

◊ Does this serve and support my highest good?

Do I Genuinely Need It?

◊ When was the last time I used this?

◊ Does it have an important and essential function in my home or life?

Does It Have a Permanent Home?

◊ Does this have a home with others of its kind?

◊ Does its home have enough space and breathing room?

◊ Is this home easy to find and easy to reach?

ACID TEST FOR ACQUIRING THINGS

1. Do I absolutely love it?

2. Do I genuinely need it?

3. What can this replace?

4. Where will its permanent home be?

SORTING

As you prepare to clear *one* drawer, pile, or area, here is a simple way to organize your stuff in its current home, on its way to a new home, or on its way out the door.

Four Piles: All the stuff you will be clearing will fall into one of these four main groups or piles:

◊ Stay

◊ Go

◊ Throw

◊ Don't Know

Sub-Piles: When you're ready, and if applicable, each pile can be further subdivided as in the following chart:

Stay	Go	Throw	Don't Know
stays put	*in-house:* transit	trash	not sure
tolerations	*out:* recycle give away sell		

Here's what these piles mean and how they work:

STAY

Stays Put Pile: This pile speaks for itself. This is the stuff that may need a little weeding and fluffing up, but it remains in its current home.

Tolerations Pile: Tolerations are useful belongings that need TLC and tasks that you've put off that need attention. Possessions that you want to keep but that need fixing, finishing, or upgrading can be set aside in the "stays put" pile or put in their own "transit" box for servicing later:

◊ anything **broken,** chipped, or that has missing parts that can be glued, sewn, nailed, replaced, repaired

◊ anything **unfinished,** such as a writing project, a sewing project, a photo project

◊ anything that **needs upgrading** or updating such as electronics, computer technologies, etc.

◊ list of tasks that require making an **appointment,** such as calling the dentist or taking the car in for an oil change

GO

Transit Pile: This is for all the things that have strayed from their permanent home. I use baskets and hooks near the stair landings to place transit items on their way home. Whenever any thing needs to go upstairs (or down), it goes into the basket. Each member of my family has his or her own basket to temporarily store personal items on their way to their permanent destination. When I'm clearing, I might also wear an apron or vest with big pockets for the smaller transit items. Transit items can fall into any of these categories:

◊ Anything that has a **home outside your home:** library books; videos that go back to Netflix; the clean platter your neighbor brought over to your potluck dinner; etc. Place this box or basket of items near the door or near your car where you can see and dispatch it most efficiently.

◊ Anything that has another **home within your home:** the tax forms on the kitchen table that need to go back to the desk in the study; tools used to repair the kitchen sink that need to return to the basement; stuff from the downstairs that needs to go back upstairs.

◊ Anything that has another **home within the same room/ space:** paid bills on the desk that belong in the file cabinet; wrapping paper on the floor that needs to be put in the box in the closet; mail on the kitchen table that needs to go into each family member's designated basket.

◊ Any toleration needing to be **serviced or fixed,** which will eventually make its way back to its permanent home.

Recycle Pile: Recycling can give new meaning and life to those things of which you're ready to let go. Each of these recycling sub-piles may require its own special box:

◊ Anything that can be **reused** or converted into something else: e.g., paper, bottles and cans, rags, tires, sneakers, metals, plastic containers, etc.

◊ Anything that might be **toxic** and must be disposed of safely: e.g., mercury thermometers, fluorescent bulbs, oil-based paints and paint thinners, car batteries, car oil, etc.

◊ Anything **large** and unwieldy that can be hauled away and used for parts: junk cars, appliances, tools, electronics, etc.

Give Away Pile: For those things that you believe still have a good "shelf life." Think about those who might enjoy or use what you no longer need or love:

- Charitable **donations:** clothing, furniture, nonperishable food, holiday cards to senior homes, paint in good condition, working cell phones for women's shelters, computers, etc.

- **Re-gifting:** items that you know will be appreciated by friends or family members

- **Kids' stuff:** durable toys, books, or clothes in good condition that your kids have outgrown

Sell Pile: This is for those things that you would like to **resell,** for example, through:

- yard sales

- online auctions, such as eBay

- consignment stores

- newspapers, community paper, or Want Advertiser

THROW

Trash Pile: Anything else that has no home in any of the three major piles gets tossed in the trash. This constitutes everything that has no life left in it and has no other place to go. Ideally, this will be the smallest of your piles. Some obvious things to throw out:

- moldy food or condiments from the refrigerator

- food in pantry that has passed its expiration date

- medicines that have passed their expiration date (which should be disposed of safely; i.e., *not* flushed down the toilet)

- anything broken that cannot be recycled for scrap (see above)

DON'T KNOW

Not Sure Pile: For anything that is a dilemma: that is, you don't know if it's a "Stay," "Go," or "Throw." You can allow yourself a short period of time to deliberate, like a week.

CLEARING PRACTICE

The practice is to clear one area of clutter combining the "four-pile" method above with the simple steps below.

Be quick and efficient, like a card dealer at a casino. Allow yourself to feel any resistance fully and completely, but don't let it slow you down or stop you.

When you're complete, close your eyes and notice how you're feeling for one minute. Notice your breathing (Is it shallow? Is it full?). Notice the energy in your body and in your space and your energy level.

CLEARING ONE AREA OF CLUTTER

1. **Identify** one area to clear and maintain strict boundaries, like police cordoning off a crime scene.

2. **Gather and Label** some boxes or baskets, and have a trash barrel on hand.

3. **Sort** the stuff into the four main piles first, sub-piles second (see chart on page 109).

4. **Clear** by using the Acid Test for Clearing described earlier in this chapter.

5. **Put Away** all items that you are keeping, beginning with "Go" and ending with "Don't Know."

CLEARING JOURNAL

As you consider the reflections below, allow yourself to feel whatever you're feeling without doing anything to fix, manage, or change it.

◊ It feels really good to address one area of clutter because _____

◊ It is easy to let go of things I don't need or use because _____

◊ What I notice about myself when I clear in a slower and more measured way is _____

◊ A pile or area that I can address today [this week] is _____

SWEEP

24

I want to be here with this moving on,
moment to moment, sweeping.
—Gunilla Norris, *Being Home*

It doesn't take much to get the energy moving, create new openings in your life, promote mindfulness, and instill a deeper caring for yourself, your home, and the world at large. But if everything you've read in this book so far is still too much to manage, or you're feeling stuck in your head, can't find a solution to a problem, or your floors are just plain dirty, my best advice is: Reach for a broom! The simple act of sweeping is energizing. It can also be soothing, meditative, and therapeutic.

CLEARING PRACTICE

Get yourself a nice broom and keep it in a prominent, handy place. Here are some ways to make friends with it.

BEFRIENDING THE BROOM

◊ **Intention:** Sweep with the intention of invoking a fresh start, creating openings in your life, clearing a path to the solution of a problem that has eluded you.

◊ **Mindfulness:** Sweep every day as a practice in mindfulness and letting go.

◊ **New Energy:** Sweep after each clearing session to bring new energy to the area cleared. Sweep your front steps to bring new energy (*chi,* or life force) through your entrance.

◊ **Expand:** Whack your mattress every six months and turn it over; shake out your bedding and hang it out to air; fluff up your sofas, chairs, pillows.

◊ **Clean:** Reach for and clear cobwebs from the ceiling, window frames, curtains, light fixtures.

◊ **Lighten Up:** Pretend that you're dancing with your beloved or playing an air guitar.

◊ **Move 'Em:** Get your lazy family off their duffs to help you!

CLEARING JOURNAL

Take a moment to reflect on your experience of using your broom.

◊ When I sweep the front steps or an area of my home, I feel _____

◊ One shift, outcome, or *ah-ha* that I've experienced as a result of sweeping with a specific intention is _____

◊ Getting the energy moving in my home, head, and heart feels good because _____

EMBRACE

25

And forgive us our trash baskets,
as we forgive those who put trash in our baskets.
**—a four-year-old's interpretation
of the Lord's Prayer, source unknown**

If it's possible to imagine an "adorable" side to clutter, it would be the three-inch tutu-clad troll pig with a missing foot that became our mascot at one of my clearing retreats.

In the workshop, I invite participants to honor their clearing process—to embrace "the beast," as it were—by bringing a small object that represents the clutter in their lives. Anything goes, as long as it's small (i.e., fits in one hand), presents a bit of a stretch to let go of, and you're willing to release it for good at the end of the program.

The Altar of Letting Go—a beautifully decorated table prominently placed at the front of the room—becomes the space holder for all the unloved and unhealed "treasures" in our homes and lives. It acts as the Witnessing Presence for everything that no longer serves and supports us.

Issues that keep you up at night, disturbances, tolerations, annoying behaviors—they all go on the table, too. I tell participants to write down on a piece of paper any issue that challenges them and place it on the table. The altar is infinitely expandable. I tell them: "She has your back. Whatever it is you're finding difficult to let go of in your life, she will take care of it for you."

By the end of the weekend, the altar begins to look a lot like those tables you see at those yard sales at the end of a long day—full of dregs you hauled up from the bowels of your basement.

Treasures that can look like this, for example:

◊ a stack of old newspapers that represent all the articles that "would illuminate me if I could only get around to reading them"

◊ a stack of legal papers (the duplicates)

◊ a stack of tourist maps and flyers "for the trip that I hope to take again someday"

◊ a pair of one-of-a-kind hand-painted designer pants that "I [yours truly] paid a fortune for"

◊ a three-inch ballerina troll-pig (minus foot)

◊ a brand-new salt and pepper shaker set, in its original box

◊ a written pledge to delete the 4,000 (still unread) emails from 2009

◊ many scraps of paper listing the thoughts and beliefs that hold us back and cause us pain

I tell everyone that this motley assortment of things isn't there to annoy us but to help us release our *attachments* to them, honor our journey, and stay awake. They also remind us to not take ourselves too seriously.

In the last hour of the course, as part of our ritual of letting go, I give each participant this instruction: "Step up to the altar and remove one or more items equal to the number of items (or challenging issues written on bits of paper) that you originally placed there." The only caveat: You cannot take back anything you brought with you.

"Choose the things that most resonated for you," I tell them, "either because its owner shared a story that touched you, it represents something you wish to clear in yourself, or it's something you want to keep. Your job when you get home is to release or enjoy it—with love."

There is a footnote to the story of our mascot. Troll Pig's foot miraculously turned up on the final morning of this particular retreat. It was the last thing to fall out of the bag of its unsuspecting owner during one of the clearing practices.

A fine footnote indeed. . . . Helping us to remember that we are whole after all.

CLEARING PRACTICE

Here's an opportunity to practice letting go of a thing or thought—with love and awareness—by following the closed-eye process below. If it helps to anchor the experience even more, consider creating a real live Altar of Letting Go.

EMBRACING AND LETTING IT GO

1. **Close** your eyes and take an easy breath in, then a slow, emptying breath out.

2. **Repeat** any or all of these phrases to help quiet the mind even more: "I am enough," "I have enough," "There is enough."

3. **Imagine** a gigantic communal Altar of Letting Go in front of you. Notice what it feels like to have a place to put things that you no longer need, use, or love.

4. **Bring awareness** to something that represents the clutter in your life that you're ready to place on your virtual altar. It can be any thing or thought that gets in the way of experiencing your best life.

5. **Release.** After you've had a chance to reflect on what that might be, imagine a higher power picking it up off the table and "handling it for you"—with love.

6. When you feel complete, **open** your eyes and reflect on the experience in your journal.

CLEARING JOURNAL

Use this space to reflect on what it means to let go, and why you can trust in the infinite support that is available to you.

◊ It is easy for me to let go of _____ because _____

◊ It is safe for me to completely surrender [*psst,* notice the feelings as you consider why it might *not* feel so "safe" to you right now] because _____

◊ It feels good to know that there is infinite support available to me (even when I clear just a teeny bit) because _____

◊ I know that I am not alone in this journey of clearing because _____

DELETE

26

How frequently does a glance at your inbox
inject you with a fresh dose of anxiety?
—Margaret Wheeler Johnson, *Huffington Post*

How did Seth Godin know that I'd be totally busted by this message he posted
on his blog one morning?

> The first thing you do when you sit down at the computer: Let
> me guess: check the incoming. Check email or traffic stats or mes-
> sages from your boss. Check the tweets you follow or the FB sta-
> tus of friends . . .

> You've just surrendered not only a block of time but your freshest,
> best chance to start something new . . .

> If you're an artist, a leader, or someone seeking to make a dif-
> ference, the first thing you do should be to lay tracks to accom-
> plish your goals, not to hear how others have reacted/responded/
> insisted to what happened yesterday.

On the day I really needed to hunker down and focus on my writing, I did
what I always do after I've had my cup of coffee: I checked my emails, the Top
News thread on Facebook, my pages on Facebook, my Twitter updates, and the
live traffic feed on my website. And did I mention the LinkedIn Group that I
started?

Big mistake.

I was looking forward to using my time well that morning. Instead, I squandered it. I allowed myself to get sucked in by a deluge of information, needs for replies, compliments, and the endlessly fascinating links to this and that.

My inbox and desktop were a screaming mess! After taking a couple of hours to put out some fires, I was a screaming mess, too. Needless to say, I got zilch done in the writing department that morning, and I was exhausted before lunch.

If you have something pressing to do or something that requires quality time, energy, concentration, creativity, or presence of mind, my best advice is to follow Seth Godin's best advice: Do *not* check emails, Facebook, Twitter (or whatever it is you plug in to) at all. Notice the resistance, *and* allow *your squirmy self to not like it.*

For all other days, the one-minute systems outlined below might help you ease into the world of technology from a more mindful and clear place. Each alone should take no longer than sixty seconds of your time. And if you manage it often, your practice can go very quickly.

It's a noisy world out there. If you have an email managing system that works for you, by all means use it!

CLEARING PRACTICE

Clear your email inbox today following the sequence of steps below with a goal of creating as much white space as possible.

CLEARING EMAIL INBOX—ONE-MINUTE DAILY MAINTENANCE

1. **Delete** any emails that require no further action. This feels really good, when you do it systematically and don't get lost in reading them.

2. **File** any emails that require no further action but need to be saved.

3. **Respond** directly to any time-sensitive emails, or flag them to look at later in the day.

4. **Follow Up Later:** Place any non-time-sensitive emails that require a response into a dedicated "Later" folder.

5. **Read Later:** Place emails that do not require a response into a dedicated "Read" folder.

6. **Watch/Listen Later:** Place all non-time-sensitive audio or video links into a dedicated "Watch/Listen" folder.

If these steps are too much to handle in one sitting, pick one and do it well—with awareness. Once you start seeing white space on a regular basis, feel free to try the suggested additional tasks below.

CLEARING EMAIL INBOX—MORE PRACTICES (TO ADD LONG TERM)

If you have the energy, inclination, and time, complete one of the tasks below. [*Psst:* Allow your "missing-out" button to get royally pressed, and notice what it feels like before, during, and after doing any of these tasks.]

1. **Unsubscribe** to one email a day that drains your energy, adds no value, and clutters your inbox.

2. **Delete** some of the Read Later or Watch/Listen Later emails.

3. **Clear** your contacts list.

CLEARING JOURNAL

Close your computer, put your phone on vibrate, and reflect on these statements below in your journal.

◊ When I can manage my email inbox in one minute or less, I feel _____

◊ It is safe for me to delete emails because _____

◊ It is safe—*and* a relief—for me not to have to read everything that I receive because _____

◊ Seeing the resulting white space in my inbox makes me feel

_____

27

DO IT

Swim out of your little pond.
—Rumi

Remember the catchy Nike print ad "Just Do It"? Listening to those inner nudges and acting on them is a powerful combination that can lead us places. You just have to know when to listen . . . then push through the lizard brain and pounce.

Like the time I nearly didn't go on my first job interview (*read:* when I am *really* glad that I pushed through my resistance and just *did it*).

It was March of my senior year in college. I had an opportunity to interview for a teaching position at one of the most selective boarding schools in the country. There was just one hitch: My appointment happened to fall on one of the snowiest days in Massachusetts that year. And I didn't have a car.

As I sat in a friend's living room stewing about how I was going to navigate the bus system sixty miles to Andover, I seriously considered bailing on the interview.

Snow. I was letting snow be the reason not to go after one of the most plum jobs a person could get. I still cringe at the thought of my twenty-two-year-old self blowing off such an incredible opportunity.

Something in me must have said *go,* because I managed to rally and haul my butt to that appointment. An appointment that led to a job offer and an experience that would reveal my true calling as a teacher and set me up with the very best tools a young person could ever hope to get.

If I had allowed a bit of inconvenience to stop me, I would not have landed the job that set the stage for every amazing opportunity that followed, which included a teaching fellowship and full scholarship that would earn me a master's degree. I am certain that I would not be where I am today if I'd not pushed through my fears on that fateful, snowy, last-chance day back in 1976.

As I reflect on that pivotal moment of my young adult life, I am also reminded of another big marker that looms just ahead: my fortieth high school reunion. What strikes me more than the fact that I've packed a lot of living into all these years in between, is that I feel like *I'm just getting started!* While some of my peers are talking about their grandchildren and retirement, I feel like I'm just now figuring out what I want to be when I grow up.

KEEP DOING IT

The truth is, this past year will go down as one of the most creative and gratifying of my life. I feel like I'm finally gaining some real clarity, traction, and momentum—realizing the full measure of what I came here to do and be. *I've got lots more I want to do!*

Though it is exciting to finally harvest some of the fruits of so much labor, I have to say, it is also a really good thing I didn't know that it would take *years* of seeding, watering, and weeding to emerge. Years of honing, editing, and pitching. Years of cursing, wailing, and wishing. Years of breaking through . . . and breaking down . . . and breaking through again.

If I could offer any wisdom about my journey so far, it would be this: If you have a passion for anything, *do it.* Now. Whether it is writing the next bestseller or keeping your email inbox moderately tamed . . .

Just do it.

Do it imperfectly and keep doing it.

Do it even if you have to claw your way up the mountain, one bloody step at a time.

Do it because we are all rooting for you to make it to the top of your Mount Everest!

Do it, not because of some desired outcome, but because *your soul depends on it.*

I, for one, will go to my fortieth high school reunion this year and wear my graying mane proudly. I will continue to surround myself with beauty, release what doesn't work for me, and keep doing what I love.

And I will continue to send out this gentle reminder to everybody out there who could use a lift and a nudge:

Do what makes your heart sing. And if you don't know what it is yet, keep going until you find it.

Or it finds you.

CLEARING PRACTICE

This is a two-minute writing exercise.

HIGHS AND LOWS

1. **Make Two Columns:** Use a blank piece of paper, or write in your journal.

2. **Left Side:** Take one minute to jot down a list of your "low-lights"—your struggles, challenges, the not-so-good feeling moments.

3. **Right Side:** Quickly download the highlights of your life—all your accomplishments, feel-good moments, and times when you were most proud of yourself (even if your actions were not reciprocated or did not visibly lead to a desired outcome).

4. **Time Yourself:** Set a timer between each side, and stop after two minutes.

5. **Dos and Don'ts:** *Do not* dwell on any of your line items, but *do* allow yourself to feel any sensations that arise and the differences in your breathing between one side and the other.

6. **Reflect:** When you've completed the above steps, take a moment to reflect in your clearing journal.

CLEARING JOURNAL

Deepen your experience of the highs and lows process by completing these statements.

◊ Some of the sensations that I experienced writing in one column versus the other include _____

◊ What I noticed about these two sides of my life was _____

◊ Some of the ways that my lowlights have informed, influenced, and led to my highlights are _____

◊ Even though it was really hard [I didn't know what I was doing; it didn't work out], I'm really glad I pushed through my resistance and followed my impulse to _____

◊ I know I am meant to realize a deeper calling to _____ (because _____)

◊ One gentle way that I can push through my resistance and *just do it* today [this week] is _____

ACTION

Small efforts applied consistently over time are the real game changer in clutter clearing.

Stress and overwhelm are signs that the fight-or-flight response has been triggered in the brain; the fight-or-flight response is useful to address immediate danger but not so useful when stepping out of our comfort zone to clear our attachments.

Every time we repeat a desired task, our brain is creating neural pathways and new "software" to support that task.

The Reduce and Repeat (R&R) method helps to bypass the fear response. It means *reducing* the perimeter and/or time spent on a task and *repeating* the same or similar task until it no longer elicits stress. The R&R method works also to address behaviors we would like to change.

A good rule of thumb for clearing is the "rule of one."

Things without a home are clutter: no home, no have.

Giving things a home recognizes their purpose and honors their value.

Sweeping, putting away, and rounding up lead to new habits and promote a sense of well-being.

Addressing one task every day is a surefire way to get the energy moving, create openings in our life, and feel really good!

PART IV

NON-IDENTIFICATION
BE THE OBSERVER

Identification . . . is a form of escape from the self.
—**Krishnamurti**

28 CLEARING WITH NON-IDENTIFICATION

Leave everything as it is in fundamental simplicity,
and clarity will arise by itself. Only by doing nothing
will you do all there is to be done.
—Khyentse Rinpoche

TO REACT OR RESPOND

I have noticed that my emotional storms have not gone away entirely, even after nearly two decades of active clearing, but they are much shorter in duration. I still have bouts during which I'll react, sometimes with a dramatic flourish that is so over the top that I might even call it pathetic. Though my ego wouldn't admit it, sometimes my reactions feel forced, like trying to jam my foot into an old shoe that no longer fits. In the midst of some category-five hurricanes, I have noticed that there is this strong witnessing part of me now that just watches with great amusement as I blow my stack.

Here's the thing: I have found that if I can allow the intensity to arise, without doing anything to fix or change it, it *does* pass.

Every moment gives us an opportunity to "be" with whatever shows up, but if a hot button gets pressed without warning, chances are we will fall back into our old small and contracted ways. Reacting or lashing out at someone because they have offended us, for example, not only keeps this particular button active, but it attracts more people and situations *(strings)* of this kind into our lives.

In the next two parts, we will explore the *non-doing* side of clearing clutter. Non-identification and Compassion are pathways that allow us to clear from a much more spacious, less attached place. They give us the means to be, in fact, *bigger than our clutter.*

CLEARING WITH NON-IDENTIFICATION

Clearing with non-identification is about witnessing. It is a guiding principle that teaches us to become the silent observers of our dramas. We don't fix anything, we don't change anything, we don't push anything. We allow fear to be fear, heartbreak to be heartbreak, guilt to be guilt, joy to be joy. We allow things to be just as they are.

Before you go into cold sweats about this accepting business, you must understand that what I refer to as "acceptance" does not mean that we tolerate the intolerable or that we don't change. It does not mean that we stand on the sidelines with our arms crossed and our noses in air, watching life pass us by without caring about or feeling a thing—quite the opposite, in fact.

Acceptance means that after you have put into motion your intentions and acted upon them responsibly, *you get out of the way* and *detach from the outcome.* You allow change, you don't force it. You feel your feelings completely and fully without owning or personalizing them. You experience weather patterns as information and feedback.

What gives the whole detachment thing its humanity is called compassion. Here in the West, where true caring is equated with doing and fixing, there is no harder lesson to be learned than this: *We cannot truly feel compassion for another person or place or being without first detaching from it!*

Non-identification is not mastered overnight. There is no quick crash course on how to unplug. There is no "getting this." This level of equanimity comes with enormous practice, dedication, and mindfulness over the course of a lifetime.

To this end, the focus of the chapters in this part will be on practice: less "doing" (as in reading) and more "being" (as in observing the mind do its thing and accepting whatever shows up).

29   ACCEPT

It just ain't possible to explain some things. It's interesting
to wonder on them and do some speculation,
but the main thing is you have to accept it—
take it for what it is and get on with your growing.
— Jim Dodge

While I waited for a jump start from AAA and realized that I was not going to make my much-needed appointment with my physical therapist, I posted this on Facebook: "*Be*-ing with the fact that my car wouldn't start this morning." Did I mention that I had made this appointment months earlier, and it was *really* hard to get?

A kind soul quickly added her empathic comment below mine: "You must be noticing the feeling that you really, really want to scream right now, right??"

Truth be told, what I was really noticing were the choices I had in this situation. Screaming was definitely one of them. Despair tinged with *poor me* was another.

Instead I opted for the "I choose ease" approach. I surprised even myself. No buttons got pressed at all.

This is progress.

BEING WITH

Practicing non-identification invites you to shift your focus. By reframing what you perceive as "yours," you can begin to change your entire relationship with a stressful pattern.

One of the ways you can practice not identifying with the physical and emotional weather patterns in your life is to simply shift your language and thoughts around them. When you can remember to do it, try replacing the subject pronoun *"I"* with the demonstrative pronoun *"This."* For instance, "I have a headache," becomes "*This is* a headache." "I'm afraid of failing" becomes "This is fear of failure." "I'm sad" becomes "This is sadness," and so on.

It may seem rather simplistic, but as one who favors simple solutions, I have found that this tool, combined with a regular diet of Softening Attitudes, is as powerful a way as any to provide an immediate shift in focus and relief.

CLEARING PRACTICE

This practice invites you to take a conscious step back from an uncomfortable thought or belief. [*Psst,* if you're dealing with a lifetime of pain and struggle, or the issue at hand holds a lot of charge, the monkey mind is probably not going to like it. Accepting things as they are when we're holding on for dear life doesn't always go down too well. This is why it's called a clearing *practice.*]

REFRAMING WITH "THIS IS"

The next time you notice yourself mouthing off another negative thought, catch yourself and replace the "I" statement with "This is. . . ." For example:

◊ *I couldn't sleep again last night* could be: "This is exhaustion," "This is weariness."

◊ *I'm sick of being everyone's slave—picking up after everyone* could be: "This is frustration," "This is despair."

◊ *The coffee tastes old:* "This is old coffee."

◊ *The dog peed on the carpet again:* "This is dog pee."

◊ *The Republicans (Democrats) are screwing us over:* "This is worry for our future."

◊ *The world is going to hell in a handbasket:* "This is fear."

After you detach in this way, notice if it brings up any emotional weather, and *feel* it fully and completely. The degree to which you allow yourself to feel the resistance (shame, guilt, pain), will dictate how quickly the weather system passes.

CLEARING JOURNAL

Use this space to deepen your experience of the process above and practice detaching even more by naming it in writing.

◊ It is safe for me to accept things just as they are because [*psst*, notice and name the part of you that *doesn't* feel so safe] _____

◊ What gets in my way of accepting things just as they are [that I would like to be more mindful of] is _____

◊ After doing the stepping back practice, I could feel _____

◊ It is safe for me to let go and trust because _____

ALLOW

30

Receive with simplicity everything that happens to you.
—Rashi

I don't know what it is about me and cars. Either the universe has a good sense of humor or knows exactly what I need to "drive home" a lesson in letting go.

Walking through the parking lot after my chiropractor's appointment the other day, I was startled to see my car—right where I had left it just forty-five minutes earlier (in perfect condition, I might add)—completely smashed in the front.

I walked around it, thinking this could not possibly be my car (it was), and this could not possibly be happening to me (it was).

The entire front bumper, hanging by one bolt, had been ripped off the chassis. There was broken glass everywhere and no note. There was no *"I'm so sorry, here's my phone number, here's my insurance information, call me, we'll make this right . . ."*

I stood there in complete disbelief.

My mind, searching for meaning and finding none, did what it does when it needs to make sense of things: it rationalizes; it has a long dueling chat with itself.

In the two hours that it took to sort out what to do, I watched my two sides—Spacious me and Poor me—duke it out:

Spacious me: Hmm, this is interesting . . .

Poor me: *OMG, my car was in a hit and run!* This *never* happens to me.

Spacious me: It could have been a lot worse . . . I could have been *in* the car.

Poor me: Such a violation! Only a brute and a coward could be so careless as to tear into the front end of this beautiful [fifteen-year-old] car and take off.

Spacious me: *He-llo? What do we have here?* There's an auto body shop right next door that I can walk to.

Poor me: It's going to cost a fortune to fix this. I have to pay for someone else's mistake?!

Spacious me: [after the lovely man from the auto body shop came to my rescue and helped me pull off the fender so that I could drive home] I'm in good hands, this guy is going to take care of my car.

Poor me: *But, but . . . I have no time for this!!*

Spacious me: Everyone is so friendly and empathetic—the lady from AAA roadside service, my insurance company handler, the police officer who wrote up the report, the gas station attendant who apologized (for not having surveillance cameras that could reach far enough to capture the accident on tape), the auto body shop angel who will fix my car . . .

On balance, dent to car and pocketbook notwithstanding, Spacious wins— if only for the rush that you feel when you are unattached to the outcome, touched by the kindness of strangers, and curious to see how it all turns out.

DUELING MINDS

The clearing practice below introduces another sibling set of the phrases that I call Softening Attitudes. Set 3 is designed to support the non-doing side of your clearing practice and bring the noisy mind back to present time (again and again).

In my own life, I have discovered how powerful this set of phrases could be when I was going through severe withdrawal from the effects of eliminating sugar, caffeine, and alcohol from my diet some years ago. Though my system did not take well to going cold turkey and went into major rebellion, it did, over time, take well to the affirming phrases below. Repeating the words silently to myself ended up being a gift of manna to my body.

It didn't start out that way, mind you. My monkey mind hated the pain and hated *be*-ing with pain: *What, do nothing?!* To the heavily attached ego-mind that wants to call the shots and is too afraid to let go for even a second, the Softening Attitudes can feel threatening. The waves of physical and emotional weather that I experienced during the first week of my cleanse showed me just how plugged up I was—both physically and emotionally.

What's more, when I leaned into the discomfort even more by asking my body to do the counterintuitive thing and *receive* the phrases like a sponge soaking up water, the net effect of *less* pain simply blew my mind. Instead of contractedness, what rushed instantly into my lower back and legs was sweet, spacious relief. And ultimate peace.

CLEARING PRACTICE

There are four phrases in set 3. Reach for them any time a button gets pressed or you feel overwhelmed, stressed, jangled, out of sorts, out of balance, or even ill.

Repeat the set with your eyes open anytime you think of them or with your eyes closed as part of a five- to twenty-minute meditation practice, and see what these phrases do for you:

I am here

I am now

I accept

I allow

1. **Begin** by finding a comfortable place to sit where you won't be interrupted for at least five minutes.

2. **Close** your eyes and settle into your chair or cushion.

3. **Insert** the first phrase of the series, "I am here," into your awareness—allowing the mind to do whatever it does.

4. **Repeat** the same phrase if you wish, or **move on** to the next one: "I am now"—noticing what it feels like.

5. **Be aware** of your breathing.

6. When you're ready, **insert** the third phrase, "I accept."

7. **Observe** thoughts and feelings without managing or controlling them in any way.

8. When you are complete, **move on** to the last phrase of the series: "I allow."

9. **Notice** the contracting and expanding effects of these phrases. Notice which ones are easier to repeat and remember. Notice which ones bring up a little hesitation or emotional weather.

10. When you feel complete, **finish** by gently wiggling your fingers and your toes; open your eyes and take a moment to reflect on your experience.

CLEARING JOURNAL

Take a moment to reflect on your experience of Simple Meditation 3 and the concept of accepting things just as they are.

◊ Before the meditation I was feeling _____ (and after _____)

◊ When I repeat the phrases "I am here" and "I am now," I feel _____

◊ When I take a step back from a stressful situation, I feel _____

◊ It is safe for me to accept and allow things to be just as they are because _____

DETACH

31

If you want there to be peace—anything from peace of mind
to peace on earth—here is the condensed instruction: stay
with the initial tightening and don't spin off. Keep it simple.
—**Pema Chödrön**

Our beloved refrigerator leaves us today. I can hear her humming away in the
other room—as she has for twenty-five years—oblivious to her fate. It's like
we're putting her down.

We bought our Hotpoint side-by-side unit in 1985, the year we were married. Back then, her creamy nubbliness and the wood-paneled vertical stripe
harmonized very nicely with the avocado stove and the linoleum floor. Save
for an occasional whine and sputter, she has never once complained and never
once needed servicing.

Why do I feel so sad? Why do I feel like such a traitor? What we're getting
to replace her is so much better for the environment . . . isn't it? We're getting a
spanking-new stainless steel model that looks really snazzy, goes with our other
appliances, and has a big energy efficiency star on it.

Attachment is not a rational thing.

CLEARING PRACTICE

This practice expands on the practices from the previous two chapters. It will
help you move through emotional weather systems quickly and fluidly. It is

designed to wear down old habits, calm the nervous system, and quiet the monkey mind.

DETACHING

The next time a button gets pressed or you feel knocked off your center—that is, you notice yourself getting rattled, hooked in, off balance, overwhelmed, sad, afraid, about ready to lose it (or you've already lost it)—proceed directly to the simple four-step process below.

To keep from getting lost or mired in emotional drama, enter into this practice with a beginner's mind. Be curious. Be gentle. Move slowly. Your concern is not *what* emerges but *how you process* the weather that arises. Follow up with another one-minute practice from this book that feels really good and is sure to lift your spirits:

1. **Stop and Breathe:** Step back with awareness. Breathe deeply. Take your breath down through your feet and ground it deep below the earth.

2. **Name and Feel:** Accept the situation just the way it is. Identify and allow your experience: for example, *"Wow, this is intense"; "This is insane"; "This is nauseating"; "This is overwhelming."* Lean into the feeling, to the degree that you're able, without personalizing it. Keep breathing.

3. **Reframe:** Exercise your power to choose differently by imagining how you wish to feel instead. Shift the focus, even if you don't quite believe (feel) the alternative. Reach for an affirmation or a Softening Attitude: for example, *"I choose ease"; "I am enough"; "I accept."* Give yourself some slack; apply a liberal dose of self-acceptance by adopting the phrasing inspired by the Emotional Freedom (Tapping) Technique: *"Even though I feel overwhelmed right now (rattled, misunderstood, vulnerable, etc.), I deeply and completely accept myself."*

4. **Repeat:** Repeat the first three steps until the weather subsides or clears.

CLEARING JOURNAL

Use the prompts below to get in touch with what your holding-on patterns look like and what it feels like to release the grip they have on you.

◊ One of the issues that I'm working through right now that I would like to release is _____

◊ What arises [physically, mentally, emotionally] when I begin to name and feel my resistance is _____

◊ What helps me to reframe the pattern is _____ (because _____)

◊ It is safe for me to let go of this issue because _____

◊ One thing that I can do for myself right now [today, this week] that would help me feel better fast is _____

32   DISAPPOINT

I live by the truth that "No" is a complete sentence.
—**Anne Lamott**

In chapter 29, "Accept," I shared the story of life throwing me a curveball and me being royally inconvenienced. What I didn't report was how I *felt* about knowing that this would royally inconvenience *someone else:* in this case, a healthcare provider who was making an extra effort to be on time. For me.

Worse than my car breaking down and me missing an opportunity to receive the care I needed, what I felt worse than anything about was that I might have disappointed my physical therapist. I could hear it in her voice when we spoke on the phone, and I watched myself going into my old familiar crawl-into-the-deepest-hole-you-can-find, cringing weather pattern.

Then I remembered an instruction I read in Cheryl Richardson's book *The Art of Extreme Self-Care* that I thought was spot on—and radical. She said that if you want to live a more authentic life, you need to (actively) learn to disappoint people.

Yes, *actively.*

Ouch. That one can be challenging for those of us who don't like to rock the boat.

If the idea of disappointing others gives you dry heaves, consider these ways to develop the muscle that will help you set clear boundaries:

- ◊ **Breathe.**
- ◊ **Decline** gracefully. You can use my favorite line for saying no: "Thanks for asking; sorry it's not going to work for me."
- ◊ **Allow** that you may have hurt someone's feelings or done something "bad."
- ◊ **Name and feel** your discomfort—guilt, self-criticism, judgment. Allow all weather to arise without taking it personally.
- ◊ **Breathe** some more.

Honestly, if you really think about it, disappointing someone is not the hard part. We unintentionally do it all the time. The harder part is doing it full on—with awareness.

CLEARING PRACTICE
ALLOWING DISCOMFORT

This practice is twofold. The first is to do something that might disappoint somebody or be hard for someone to hear, such as saying no or speaking your truth. The second is to reflect in your journal what it *feels* like. Remember that naming and feeling the discomfort is a form of clearing too.

CLEARING JOURNAL

Use this space to name and feel any weather that comes up around disappointing others.

- ◊ Someone [something] I would like to say no to is _____
- ◊ The idea of saying no [speaking my truth] makes me feel _____
- ◊ Some of the emotional weather and resistance that arise when I consider how I may have disappointed a friend [family member] from my past is _____
- ◊ Saying no supports my highest and best self because _____

33 DON'T IDENTIFY

You are the sky. Everything else—it's just the weather.
—Pema Chödrön

How many times have you gone into a big warehouse store feeling just fine and come out feeling totally depleted? Or maybe you're standing in the checkout line of your supermarket and suddenly feel a wave of emotion, such as depression, worry about money, anxiety—something you weren't feeling before. Perhaps you walk into a room and feel disturbed for no particular reason.

After nearly two decades of clearing the energetic equivalent of clutter in people's spaces, here is what I know for sure: Most of the stress we feel in our lives *isn't even ours!*

If this statement seems farfetched, let me bend your mind even more when I say that most of what humans perceive as physical and emotional stress is an unconscious reaction to invisible energies that swirl in the ether. Our living spaces are a lot like a deep-sea experience: They are alive and teeming with energy signatures that may or may not feel friendly to us, depending on how we relate to them (i.e., how aware, attached, and fearful we are).

When *a* headache (that you were not feeling moments earlier) becomes *my* headache, *a* sadness becomes *my* sadness, or *a* worry becomes *my* worry, you can bet that you've just identified with a stressful pattern, decided it was yours, and taken it home with you.

So how do we not "take home" the guck that we feel that is not ours to begin with? You can start first by being more accepting of things as they are and personalizing less—as Eckhart Tolle reminds us in this interview that I happened to catch on ABC's *Nightline* late one night:

> *Nightline:* Don't you ever get annoyed, irritated, or sad—anything negative?
>
> Eckhart Tolle: No, I accept what is; that's why life has become so simple.
>
> *Nightline:* Even when somebody cuts you off in your car?
>
> Eckhart Tolle: It's fine. It's like a sudden gust of wind. I don't personalize a gust of wind. It's simply what is.

So the next time you're in a big warehouse store, standing in line, waiting to be served at a restaurant, or hanging out in someone's home or workplace, notice how you feel in the space. Do you feel the same or different from how you did before you arrived? Do you feel energized or tired? Does it make a difference if you move to the other side of the space or the room? How's your breathing?

The degree to which you can be aware and not personalize any discomfort you feel as you move about your life, that's when it, and *you,* change—for good.

CLEARING PRACTICE

Stress patterns that are not ours become ours the instant we *identify* with them. This is a simple practice that will help you detach from any issue or weather that you find uncomfortable.

NOT IDENTIFYING

The next time you suddenly feel a wave or pang of something that you weren't feeling just moments before, take an easy breath in and out as you repeat this phrase quietly to yourself: "It's not mine."

Notice how it feels to take a step back and watch the sensations that are stirred without getting stuck or lost in their drama.

CLEARING JOURNAL

Use this space to reflect on times when you have gotten plugged in by a thing, place, or person and how it feels to take one step back and not identify with it.

◊ One of the ways that I feel myself getting plugged in by [a thing, location, person] is _____

◊ What I can do immediately when I notice myself taking on, or getting sucked in by, an unsavory energy that I wasn't feeling moments before is _____

◊ When I repeat "It's not mine," I notice myself _____

◊ It is safe for me to detach from an issue that I was feeling today because _____

ALLOW MYSTERY

34

Embrace your confusion. Let there be peace
in not knowing all the answers.
—Cheryl Richardson, *Self-Care Cards*

Yesterday I went from being on top of the world to being at the bottom in less than two hours. From the highest of the high to crash and burn in no time flat.

It was the day that a huge email blast went out announcing the release of the previous incarnation of *Your Spacious Self:* a gorgeous email sent out by a prominent messenger on my behalf to his list of tens of thousands of people.

The day started out with a bang: a thrilling adrenaline rush of page clicks, email series subscriptions, sales on Amazon. All the metrics were looking really good. Years and years of writing, preparing, designing, getting all my ducks in a row, and I was cruisin'—finally getting my moment in the sun; giving my book the big launch it deserved.

It was like watching my horse racing into first place way ahead of the pack, with all my money in . . .

Until my horse came to a grinding halt, stopped dead in her tracks—just like that.

The server that I use to host my website inexplicably crashed. All links and page access snapped shut like a clam for the rest of the day. The gig was over.

I was incredulous. Punched out. Defeated. Left high and dry in the middle of my not knowing, with my winning ticket hanging limp in my hands.

How could this happen? Why would the universe tease me then let me down like this?

Then miraculously, from some dark corner in the "temple" of Facebook (of all places), came this post from one of my favorite spiritual teachers, Pema Chödrön. With those compassionate eyes and smile looking down upon me, she had a message for me, direct from the Big U, which I excerpt below:

> Anxiety, heartbreak, and tenderness mark the in-between state. It's the kind of place we usually want to avoid. . . . Becoming intimate with the queasy feeling of being in the middle of nowhere only makes our hearts more tender. When we are brave enough to stay in the middle, compassion arises spontaneously. By not knowing, not hoping to know, and not acting like we know what's happening, we begin to access our inner strength.

I bawled my eyes out. Of course! How could I not remember this? I write about not knowing in the book.

But I forgot. I got greedy. I was lost in self-importance, caught in the spin cycle of agenda, control, and small-mindedness. The universe was giving me a huge assist by pulling the plug.

The server is running again. Website is up. All systems humming along.

I have no idea how many book purchases, new email subscription sign-ups, or Facebook "Likes" I might have received had this technical glitch (and my meltdown) never happened.

Something tells me that in all its exquisite messiness, my big launch day played itself out perfectly. If only to let me know that things always work out even better when I get out of the way . . . and accept that not everything is what it seems.

HANGING OUT WITH "NOT KNOWING"

Quitting the career and job that defined me for two decades led to a long period of fumbling in the foggy netherworld that I call Not Knowing. I still find myself visiting that place from time to time. These moments come on when I might least expect them and often when something new is about to be born. I never know how long these periods will last, but they have become like old friends that I do my best to welcome into my life.

When you make space in your life—by conscious choice or not—you are likely to enter a period of deep unknowing, where nothing you do or experience makes any sense in the context of what preceded it; where your vital connections seem completely lost. You may even hit the proverbial wall and splatter all over the floor, as I have done so many times in my life.

Allow the mystery. Feel its twists and turns and seeming dead ends. This is a very fertile place in which to hang out if you can bear the uncertainty and discomfort of it. I have found these periods in my life to be powerful and creative—dark and messy and exasperating a lot of the time but rich, like black soil that fosters new growth.

CLEARING PRACTICE
MAKING FRIENDS WITH NOT KNOWING

Is there something going on in your life right now that doesn't quite add up? Is there an issue that eludes you or remains unsolved or unclear? A person you just can't quite figure out? A situation that leaves a bad taste in your mouth, and you can't put your finger on it?

Use this opportunity to do nothing more than *hang out in a place of not knowing;* to lean into it to the degree that you can handle it.

What arises for you when you detach from an outcome?

CLEARING JOURNAL

Use your journal to deepen your experience of not knowing.

◊ Some of the issues in my life that I find uncomfortable [can't figure out] are _____

◊ What I feel when I lean into the experience of not knowing even more is _____

◊ It is safe for me to enter into a period of not knowing because _____

◊ One thing I can do right now [today, this week] to ease my discomfort around not knowing [the answer, my next step] is _____

Non-identification

35 DO NOTHING

Sometimes I sits and thinks, and sometimes I just sits.
—Satchel Paige, American baseball player

Why is it that whenever someone catches us doing nothing, we immediately jump to our feet so that we're not perceived as total time-wasting deadbeats? If this is something you can relate to, here's a radical idea for your mind to chew on: Doing nothing is a legitimate state of being.

If you're a big doing machine, like most people, my guess is that this idea isn't going to sit well. Especially if you live in the West, where all accomplishment and achievement are measured by how well we "do."

Non-doing is like a big empty hall that you hang out in for a while. Doesn't sound all that inviting, but here's what I know: Practicing doing nothing for a few minutes every day opens us up to a whole new side of ourselves that we didn't know was there.

Here are some ways to make friends with it:

◊ Do nothing while waiting in line.

◊ Do nothing while sitting at a red light.

◊ Do nothing while waiting for dinner to be cooked or the tea water to boil.

◊ Do nothing when the phone rings.

◊ Do nothing when you would typically reach for something to do, such as watch TV, check Facebook, text a friend.

You may discover a yummy spaciousness, a quiet stillness, a deep peace—a blissful space that doesn't feel cold or empty at all!

CLEARING PRACTICE

UNDOING

You guessed it. Your practice, if you choose to accept it, is to do nothing at all and notice what *that* feels like.

Notice the impulse to do. Notice and allow the restlessness, the queasiness, the fretfulness—and ride it out.

Notice your breathing.

When you feel complete, go to your journal and reflect on your experiences.

CLEARING JOURNAL

Use this space to reflect on what it feels like to do absolutely nothing.

◊ Having empty space in my life feels _____

◊ It feels good [doesn't feel good] to do nothing because _____

◊ It is safe for me to be caught doing nothing because _____

◊ Some of the ways that I can cultivate "more nothing" in my life are _____

NON-IDENTIFICATION

Non-identification is pure witnessing.

Pure witnessing means that we don't analyze, personalize, or get lost in any emotional weather patterns.

Non-identification is a state of being that we cultivate and practice.

What gives detachment its humanity is called "compassion."

We cannot hold a space of true compassion for another being without first detaching.

Detaching makes physical clearing much easier.

Mystery is a legitimate state of being.

Hanging out in "not knowing" is letting go.

Letting go is clearing.

PART V

COMPASSION
FEEL GOOD NOW

If you want others to be happy, practice compassion.
If you want to be happy, practice compassion.
—**Dalai Lama**

36 CLEARING WITH COMPASSION

> We do not have to improve ourselves;
> we just have to let go of what blocks our heart.
> —Jack Kornfield

SURELY JOY

In the town of Concord, Massachusetts, where Henry David Thoreau lived and mused about life, I came across these words by the man himself on a bumper sticker on a beat-up old car: "Surely joy is the condition of life." I stopped and smiled and wrote it down. It has been dancing around in my consciousness ever since.

Surely joy is the condition of life. I swirl it like a glass of fine wine. I smell its bouquet. I savor it slowly like a meal that reveals more of its mystery and perfection with each bite. I swoon over it like pure ambrosia. Hmmm. Can it be so easy?

"Surely joy . . . Sounds like someone's name," my husband later remarked over dinner, like "Shirley Joy." I'm thinking, "Yeah, like someone you love to spend time with because she's fun and playful and laughs a lot; she 'gets you' completely and is totally unconditional with her praise and excitement for you." Shirley is the total opposite of control freak Hilda, whose name I coined years ago to identify that side of me that I'm not particularly proud of—Hilda, short for "Hard-on-Yourself-Hilda."

Weigh the two with both palms up: Hmmm, Hard-on-Yourself-Hilda? Shirley Joy? Which one sounds like someone *you'd* like to hang out with?

The thing about clutter is that it has no sense of humor. It doesn't know a thing about joy. Joy is not within its scope or in its vocabulary. Compared to joy, clutter is one dimensional. Distracting. Complicated. Dull and flat.

Joy. It is the byproduct of clearing. It is the champagne bubbles of being spacious. It is the natural flow that springs out of clarity. It is the fountain of youth. It is unstoppable, eternal, attractive, magnetic. It is the energy we give off when we are clear.

Joy is who we are.

So if you're thinking, how do I get some—or more—of *that,* let's just say that we've been building up to it slowly.

In the previous three parts—Intention, Action, and Non-identification—you have had the opportunity to practice focusing attention, taking action baby steps, and detaching from any drama that arises. In this part, we will explore the fourth clearing pathway: *compassion.* Compassion is the softening balm of the clearing process, the part that connects you to your source of pure guidance, supports effortless release, and allows pure joy to simply bubble up.

Compassion, as in, *with* passion.

CLEARING WITH COMPASSION

One of my biggest revelations in my journey has been this one: It's all well and good to feel our feelings to their full and natural completion, but if we don't feel safe as we clear our clutter, *we will not budge an inch.* What we need is a container that allows us to feel safe enough to let go. In space clearing, it is the practitioner who provides the safe container for the client and the space to release holding patterns. In clutter clearing, that container is called self-care.

To those for whom compassion conveys an ideal of selflessness—the altruistic quality that we all aspire to (and brings up all of our inadequacies when we haven't lived up to the level of perfection that it implies)—allow me to clarify.

My focus is on the concept of "self-fullness": as in self-love, self-worth, self-acceptance. It means being kind and forgiving, as in giving yourself massive amounts of slack; allowing yourself to disappoint and be disappointed; having it be okay to mess up and fail; setting clear boundaries. Without nourishing self-care, there is no clearing. Period. Nor true spaciousness, for that matter. Clearing with compassion is "holding a space" for yourself.

Compassion is the clearing pathway that helps us feel safe enough to let go. Held in compassion, feelings of grief or shame, for example, will lose their charge and reorganize naturally into something more spacious, more coherent. Watch a mother hold her disconsolate child without conditions or an agenda or a need to fix or do anything, and you get the idea. The child walks away feeling all better because his mom simply held a space for him. We can cultivate this level of safety only when we support and believe in ourselves implicitly.

Think of the Mother Teresa quality *in you*. That part in you that is big enough to feel the worst weather and still not be affected by it. The part that smiles with a permanent twinkle in its eye. The ability to act as your own "witnessing presence" is what it means to clear with compassion.

If you feel undersupported or malnourished in the self-care department, part 5 offers a banquet of opportunities to feed your soul. They will become particularly important and useful if and when you experience any uncomfortable side effects from clearing the clutter in your life.

REST

37

How beautiful it is to do nothing, and then rest afterward.
—Spanish proverb

Rest. Doesn't that sound simply divine?

If it's so delicious, why is it that we don't put our feet up and close our eyes more often? Winston Churchill is famous for his afternoon catnaps. Siesta time has been a main staple of the Spanish culture for centuries, and most businesses close their doors every afternoon. It doesn't seem to affect their productivity one bit.

The benefits of sleep, of course, are well documented. It repairs and restores balance to the body, boosts the immune system, promotes longevity, recharges our batteries, beautifies, and elevates!

Research shows that napping from twenty to sixty minutes increases brain connectivity, decision making, problem solving, and creativity. Vèronique Vienne, in her inspiring book *The Art of Doing Nothing,* has a lot to say on the benefits of taking naps:

> Sleep research shows that below the surface of a peaceful snooze, a complex physiological process is taking place. . . . While we sleep, sophisticated sequences of brain waves transform our inert bodies into humming power stations that produce intelligence, alertness, and discernment. . . . Surrendering to slumber does more than just restore the ability to function efficiently—it actually generates that clear and transparent state of mind we call wakefulness.

Yes, wakefulness—as in an expanded state of consciousness—that fabulous byproduct of clutter clearing that we've been talking about since page one.

The next time you think that you're just catching a few z's, consider that you are also sending a powerful message about creating space for yourself—for downtime, slow time, soul time.

What do you say? How about making a little time today to close your eyes? Get up from where you are sitting. Close the office door. Find a park bench. Curl up somewhere and relax. Once you've found your spot, wiggle around in it until you feel perfectly supported in a state of utter *ahhh*.

Or just sit right where you are, close your eyes, and infuse yourself with the simple meditation offered below.

CLEARING PRACTICE

This practice presents the fourth and last set in the series of Softening Attitudes.

Practice these anytime you're feeling stressed, overwhelmed, or exhausted. Use them to help cultivate self-care and compassionate awareness.

Repeat the set with your eyes open anytime you think of them or with your eyes closed as part of a five- to twenty-minute meditation practice.

> I rest in stillness
>
> I rest in awareness
>
> I rest

SIMPLE MEDITATION 4—REST

1. **Begin** by finding a comfortable place to sit, and be sure to "wiggle around" until you feel supremely comfortable.

2. **Close** your eyes and take a long, easy breath in, then a slow, emptying breath out.

3. **Insert** the first phrase of the series, "I rest in stillness," into your conscious awareness—allowing the mind to do whatever it does.

4. **Repeat** the same phrase if you wish, or move on to the next phrase, "I rest in awareness," noticing what it feels like.

5. When you feel complete, **move on** to the third phrase: "I rest."

6. **Allow** your thoughts and feelings to arise without doing anything to fix or manage them. Notice your breathing.

7. When you feel complete, **finish** by gently wiggling your fingers and your toes; open your eyes and take a moment to reflect on your experience.

CLEARING JOURNAL

Take a moment to reflect on your experience of the fourth simple meditation and how it feels to cultivate and experience stillness and deep rest.

◊ Before the meditation I was feeling _____ (and after _____)

◊ When I repeat these phrases, I feel _____

◊ When I allow myself to drop into a state of deep stillness, I feel _____

◊ What gets in the way of my experiencing deep rest is [*psst,* note the impulse to blame someone else or something external; use this as an opportunity to explore what *you do* to get in your own way] _____

◊ It is safe for me to grow very still and spacious because _____

38 NOURISH

Whenever you are sincerely pleased, you are nourished.
— Ralph Waldo Emerson

DRINKING WATER IS CLEARING

I must sound like a broken record when it comes to asking how you are feeling and whether or not your breathing is shallow or relaxed—two of the best ways I know to tune in to and support the body as it decodes and processes stressful information in the environment "out there."

I should add to the drill: Are you thirsty?

The reason for this question is that clearing physical, mental, and emotional clutter is very dehydrating.

There is a lot going on behind the scenes as we process and release our attachments. In my experience of clearing, a (really good) sign that we are moving stuck energy is thirst.

Drinking good, pure water is like hitting the refresh button on your body, and it's a great way to ease the side effects of clearing.

I'm no scientist, but here's what I know about water and the lack of it:

◊   Most of us are dehydrated, and we don't even know it.

◊   Our bodies are made up mostly of water; the leaner we are, the more water we are.

◊   We need to drink half of our body weight in ounces every day to stay fully hydrated. If you weigh 150 pounds, for example, this means drinking about nine cups a day (or seventy-two ounces). For therapeutic benefits, increase this ratio by 20 to 40 percent.

◊ Chugging two glasses of water first thing in the morning flushes out toxins. I'm told you have to chug, not sip, to get the most benefit.

◊ Not all water is created equal. Some of the expensive bottled water is very acidic (as opposed to alkaline on the pH scale), which, like eating certain foods, creates free radicals in the body.

◊ Free radicals are molecules that are missing an electron. Like little hungry Pac Man junkies, free radicals roam the body looking to bond with, and feast on, our healthy tissues and organs.

◊ We don't die, we oxidize. To put it more crassly, we rust. If you wonder what that looks (or feels) like as we get older, think joint pain and wrinkles. Everything we do, including exercise and plain old breathing, is a natural process of oxidation.

◊ Drinking good alkaline water detoxifies, reverses the aging process, lubes the joints, and is energizing.

◊ Increasing your intake of good water brings the glow back into your face . . . and life. Who needs all those expensive face creams and remedies to combat stress when we can reach for good water instead!

EATING REAL FOOD IS CLEARING

It is not just water that you need to think about. To fuel and support a daily clearing practice, you need to upgrade your food to *real* food.

Michael Pollan, bestselling author of *Omnivore's Dilemma,* said it best with his (now famous) seven words: "Eat food, not too much, mostly plants." This means eating foods that you can cook and pronounce: whole grains, fruits, vegetables, fish, meat.

Pollan elaborates with these (also famous) seven rules for eating, which I paraphrase here:

◊ Don't eat anything your great-grandmother wouldn't recognize as food.

◊ Don't eat anything with more than five ingredients or ingredients you can't pronounce.

◊ Stay away from the middle of the supermarket; shop along the perimeter of the store where the real food is located (and easily replaced when it goes bad because of its proximity to the loading docks).

◊ Don't eat anything that won't eventually rot. Things like Twinkies that never go bad are not food. The only exception— a food that doesn't go bad that *is* good for you—is honey.

◊ Don't buy food where you buy your gas. Twenty percent of food in the US is consumed in a car.

◊ Always leave the table a little hungry, or, as the German saying goes, "Tie off the sack before it is full."

◊ Enjoy meals with the people you love.

What is one fake food choice that you could replace with one real food choice? That would be a very good place to start.

CLEARING PRACTICE
NOURISHING

This is an opportunity to notice what it feels like (physically and energetically) when you change the quantity and quality of the water you drink and the food you eat. [*Psst,* if you keep the changes small for both water intake and new food choices, you'll be less likely to rebel.]

◊ **Water:** Start by drinking eight more ounces of water a day than you usually do, and increase by that amount every day [week] until you reach the minimum recommended amount (of half your body weight in ounces). It helps to measure out the exact amount of water in a clear jug so that you can be sure you're meeting your goal. If you're committed to making a change in your life, consider increasing your intake of water by 20 to 40 percent.

◊ **Food:** Start with this sensing exercise: Eat a (whole) food item that makes you swoon and nourishes you alongside a food item that has no nutritional or taste value whatsoever. Touch and smell each before they go into your mouth. Chew them well. Notice what each tastes like. Compare the energetic effects of the two on your body before, during, and several hours after eating. Based on your findings, consider upgrading your diet by replacing, in small increments, one food choice that does not nourish you with one that does.

Record your impressions (physical, mental, emotional) in your journal.

CLEARING JOURNAL

Use this space to explore what it feels like to support and nourish your body.

◊ What I'm noticing about increasing my water intake (besides having to go the bathroom more) is _____

◊ When I compare a food that nourishes me with one that does not add any value [in terms of smell, feel, and taste], I notice _____

◊ It is easy for me to make incremental changes to my diet because [*psst,* notice your resistance] _____

◊ Some of the changes that I am seeing in my home and life as a result of changing what I put into my body are _____

◊ Starting today, I commit to supporting my body in these ways: _____

39 SUPPORT

Support equals release.
—**Svaroopa yoga tenet**

I practice a very gentle style of yoga called Svaroopa. Supported poses that utilize a variety of props to achieve specific angles in the body are a Svaroopa hallmark. These poses are especially designed to promote a state of deep relaxation by releasing core tensions, which are said to radiate from tight muscles surrounding the tailbone. After years of experimenting with all kinds of yoga, some of which I've loved, I discovered the one style that not only helped me feel good fast (without sore muscles or injury), but gave me a direct and doable way to practice the thing that this book is all about: *letting go.*

Think of a time when you felt unconditionally supported, even for a brief moment. Can you remember what it felt like? Perhaps it was your partner surprising you with coffee in bed or your boss giving you the rest of the day off or your daughter giving you a shoulder massage.

Though it's a wonderful thing when it happens, being unconditionally supported requires a very spacious human to supply it. What I love about my daily yoga practice is that it delivers support on the spot—and a *lot* of return for very little effort.

Every morning at the start of my day, I'll lie on the floor and place a number of thick, rolled-up blankets under my knees to keep my spine completely flat. Sometimes, when I cannot drag myself out of bed, I'll put a bolster under my knees and do the pose right then and there. It's a wonderful way to transition into my day.

Once settled in this perfect alignment, the muscles in my body, beginning at the tailbone, will soften and relax. After a few minutes, I feel deliciously spacious, as I do when I've had a deep massage. If I can stay present, the result of such simple support is nothing short of heaven on earth.

There are other fabulous Svaroopa poses that I do (in a chair) throughout the day, as well, to release the buildup of tightness in my neck and shoulders from sitting at my computer all day.

Apply the principle of support to *any* aspect of your life, and you might achieve miraculous levels of spaciousness on every level. The clearing practice below is one way to invite effortless release—and *real ease.*

SUPPORT EQUALS REAL EASE

For the purposes of clearing clutter and giving you a yummy taste of support, I have adapted a simple pose that I do myself every day at home. It can be practiced anywhere and requires no previous yoga experience. The secret is in the setup and positioning of your body. With correct alignment, you allow gravity to do all the opening work for you. This practice goes really well with any of the four simple meditations presented in this book.

There is one (big) *caveat:* I am not a certified yoga instructor, and this pose alternative is not intended to replace the real thing. For that, I highly recommend you check out a Svaroopa yoga class in your city or hometown. Nothing beats it for what it can do to support a regular clearing practice that feels good and lasts a lifetime.

CLEARING PRACTICE

Practice the Floor Pose by following the steps indicated below.

THE FLOOR POSE

This pose is a quick way to relieve stressful buildup, decompress, and/or start your day. It does not replace what I consider to be the "Cadillac of support"—

which uses a bevy of rolled-up blankets and bolsters in the true Svaroopa style. In the absence of a class and props, I have found this pose to be a suitable alternative. As the name suggests, it requires a floor (I recommend a mat or carpet, as well). You will also need a chair, sofa, or bed to complete this variation.

Here's how to do it:

1. **Begin:** Lie down on a floor next to a chair, sofa, or bed.

2. **Position:** Bend both knees, and place your lower legs squarely on the chair, sofa, or bed, insuring that your spine is completely flat on the floor from your tailbone to your head.

3. **Adjust:** If the chair, sofa, or bed is too high to achieve a flat spine, place a folded blanket or two under your body. If these surfaces are too low, you can raise your legs by placing a folded blanket or two under them.

4. **Fine-Tune:** Draw your chin in slightly to lengthen the spine. Place a small pillow under your head if you need one to achieve this.

5. **Release:** Once positioned, relax completely (i.e., let go).

6. **Finish** *(important)***:** To come out of this pose, turn your body over on one side and *slowly* push yourself up with both arms.

7. **Integrate:** Allow your body to integrate the effects of the pose by sitting (or lying) quietly for a few breaths.

CLEARING JOURNAL

Take a moment to reflect on ways that you can receive support in your life and how you already do.

◊ It is safe for me to be deeply supported in my life because _____

◊ I am worthy of receiving support in my life because _____

◊ After practicing the Floor Pose, I feel _____

◊ Other ways that I can support letting go and invite real ease in my life are _____

REFRESH

40

Let the past drift away in the water.

—Japanese saying

Most people I know seem to love the energizing boost of a morning shower. I much prefer to bathe at night before I go to bed. Even if I'm dog tired and can barely keep my eyes open, I'll drag a toothbrush and a string of dental floss across my teeth and take a shower. The idea of climbing into a clean bed while still dirty from my day feels icky to me. Showering at night helps me sleep better, too.

Bathing right before I go to bed clears me of my day. It releases some of the "stringy" buildup and helps me gather all the scattered parts of myself. If I have the luxury of time, need some extra help unwinding, or I feel chilled, I'll run a hot bath, add a mix of sea salt and baking soda, and soak in that for a while.

Mixing salt and soda in water—to soak in or as a body rub in the shower—offers the additional benefit of mitigating the energetic side effects associated with clearing. It is wonderfully restorative, detoxifying, and integrating. It helps to restore balance anytime you feel out of sorts, depleted, or just plain stuck.

SALT AND SODA BATH OR SHOWER

This simple formula was adapted from an old Edgar Cayce remedy by my friend, Bay-area teacher and healer Desda Zuckerman. She recommends pure, coarse sea salt (instead of Epsom salts).

◊ Combine equal parts coarse sea salt (or Kosher salt) with Arm and Hammer (or similar brand) baking soda.

◊ For a shower (after you've shampooed, soaped, and rinsed off), make a paste in your palm and rub it all over your body, including your hair, then shower off.

◊ For a hot bath, simply pour the mixture into the tub and soak.

◊ It doesn't matter if it's a cup to a cup or a teaspoon to a teaspoon, as long as it's *equal parts* of sea salt and soda.

I buy my coarse sea salt in bulk at my local natural foods store and the baking soda in the ten-pound bag they sell at Costco, which lasts me a long while. I mix a four-cup batch at a time (two cups of each) in a jar and keep it next to the tub. Both salt and soda have a way of absorbing all kinds of unsavory energies, so make sure the bags are well sealed before you store them.

CLEARING PRACTICE
REFRESHING

Take a salt and soda shower or bath following the recipe and instructions above. Even if you are a morning bather, try it at least once before bedtime after a round of clutter clearing and/or after a long day.

Notice the effects on your energy level, in particular.

CLEARING JOURNAL

Use this space to reflect on the physical and energetic shifts from adding salt and soda to your regular bathing routine.

◊ After taking a salt and soda shower [bath] I noticed _____

◊ What I notice about bathing before going to bed at night is _____

◊ Other ways that I can support and honor myself in letting go are _____

SPEND TIME ALONE

41

A little while alone in your room will prove more valuable than anything else that could ever be given you.
—Rumi

I love spending time alone. And I need it like a plant needs water and sun.

Last summer, I used some solo time to restore a couple of rooms that had been emptied for a much-needed paint job. The smaller of the two rooms housed our entire library of books (*read:* hundreds of dusty volumes, some of which have not seen the light of day in nearly two decades).

So I got to do my favorite thing: play my music really loud and redecorate, which, for me, means thinking about each item (*Do I love it? Will I use it again?*) and placing things . . . changing my mind . . . and placing them again (and again until it feels right). I needed every second of all three days to complete the task in a way that was fun and honored my measured and organic process.

Though I usually love the boon of two or three days of unscheduled time alone, and crave it even, the longer stretches are not always a panacea. I notice that too much time alone has a sneaky way of bringing up some old baggage that produces anxiety and loneliness. When I feel this way, it helps me to go outside, get together with a friend, call someone.

Even if the thought of time alone feels radical or produces anxiety for you, I hope this chapter inspires you to try it by doing something you love—without hesitation or apology.

One of the recommendations Julia Cameron makes in her book *The Artist's Way* is to take yourself out on a solo date. Yes, treat yourself to lunch, a concert, a museum—anything that makes your heart sing. I took myself out to dinner and the theatre once when I was doing the lessons in her book. What I noticed, besides it being surprisingly fun, is that on such short notice, I was able to get one of the best seats in the house.

CLEARING PRACTICE
CULTIVATING ALONE TIME

Take out your calendar and schedule a time to take yourself on a date sometime in the next week. You can plan ahead or be spontaneous. Go out, or stay home when the rest of the family is away.

And remember: "By yourself" means *for* your self.

CLEARING JOURNAL

Use this space to reflect on what it feels like to spend time alone and how to cultivate that time.

◊ When I am alone and doing what I love, I feel _____

◊ What gets in the way of me getting the alone time that I need is _____

◊ My favorite place to be when I'm alone is _____

◊ It feels safe for me to spend time alone because _____

◊ The next time the family is away, I will commit to honoring myself by _____

ASK FOR HELP

42

Cooperation, and not competition,
may be nature's most fundamental operating principle.
—Tom Shadyac

My lower back spazzed out last summer while I was helping my husband assemble the large pieces that would become the new Adirondack chairs for the patio.

One mindless lift of a chair part, one split second of searing pain, and boom, it's over: I'm out of commission for days. Couldn't even lift a spoon after it had happened.

I know exactly how it happened, too. Two industrial-sized boxes had been sitting like unwelcome squatters in our backyard for weeks—taking up lots of (mind) space. I was on a tear to finally get them out of there and finish the job: open the gigantic boxes, remove the Styrofoam, pull out the chair parts (which weighed a ton), line up the tools, make room for us to work. I was doing what I always do when I'm in task mode: dive in, exert, push, make it happen, ignore the body's limitations (and consider my options instead), dismiss the cautionary whisperings to slow down, and forget to ask for help.

Ask for help.

Oh yes, *that*. Those three words that take no time to utter but have a way of sending my supercompetent, *I-can-do-it-better-and-faster* self into spasms of resistance—real ones—now throbbing in my lower back.

Why am I so allergic to asking for help?

It could well be because I was raised to fend for myself. Many firstborns like myself are very good at this. And birth order, in my case, will show up sometimes as the tough-as-nails sidekick, Hard-on-Yourself-Hilda, piping in with her usual shrill thoughts:

◊ **Soldier On:** You must soldier on, no matter what, because people depend on you [and God forbid the world might stop functioning properly if you don't take care of it/them now].

◊ **Do It Yourself:** You must do it yourself—and multiple variations such as: you cannot trust or rely on anyone to do it as well as you can; being on the receiving end of the equation means you're weak; your staying alert and anxious helps others do their job better (like fly airplanes, drive taxis).

◊ **Don't Disappoint:** Letting someone down and disappointing people is really bad. Better to tell a lie than say something authentic and truthful that would make you feel uncomfortable.

◊ **It's Not Okay:** It's not acceptable to leave things incomplete, unfinished, or messy; it's not okay to not know; it's not okay to do nothing.

That Hilda. She's a piece of work.

HARDWIRED FOR COMPASSION

The truth is, self-sufficiency is a good skill to have when you're traveling alone in a remote area or being stalked by lions in the savannah. In a world full of people—many of whom are not only eager to lend a hand, but wired for it—why is it that we don't tap into this valuable human resource?

In a quest to answer the fundamental question: "What is wrong with our world and what can we do about it?" movie director Tom Shadyac shares the revelation that came out of the making of his provocative documentary, *I AM*:

> Science is discovering a plethora of evidence about our hardwiring for connection and compassion, from the vagus nerve, which releases oxytocin at simply witnessing a compassionate act, to

the mirror neuron, which causes us to literally feel another person's pain. Darwin himself, who was misunderstood to believe exclusively in our competitiveness, actually noted that humankind's real power comes in their ability to perform complex tasks together, to sympathize and cooperate.

My Hilda may not be entirely on board with all of this—yet. We're working on it.

CLEARING PRACTICE
REACHING OUT

On a piece of paper or in your clearing journal, create three columns. At the top, write the words "Need," "Contact," and "By." Then follow these steps:

1. **Begin:** Think of one to five issues that could use some outside (or inside) help.

2. **Brainstorm:** In the "Need" column, state your issue in one sentence or less. In the "Contact" column, brainstorm who might be able to support you. Include the phone number, email address, or website if it helps. In the "By" column, set a reasonable time frame for yourself.

3. **Prioritize:** Put a number 1 next to the first call you need to make, a 2 to indicate the next task, and so on.

4. **Simplify:** Keep the tasks simple and doable. If this exercise makes you feel overwhelmed, adopt the R&R method: reduce your list, and repeat the task.

5. **Feel:** Notice how it feels before, during, and after this exercise. Notice your breathing. Notice if you're feeling thirsty.

Your list might look something like this:

Need	Contact	By	
Make plane reservations	Jet Blue	June 30	3
Change oil	Call T & F guys	Now	1
Rearrange closet	Closet organizer	Friday	2

CLEARING JOURNAL

After you have created your support list, reflect on the statements below.

◊ I know I need help with _____

◊ It is easy for me to consider asking for help because _____

◊ Some of the emotional weather that comes up for me when I consider asking for support [having someone see my home, having someone work on my body, talking to a housemate, etc.] is _____

◊ It is safe for me to step out of my comfort zone and seek help because _____

◊ It is necessary for me to get help now because _____

LIGHTEN UP 43

Ever since happiness heard your name,
it has been running through the streets trying to find you.
—Hafiz

Sometimes life delivers a perfect storm of disasters that are so bad they're funny. It's almost like the universe is doing a koochie-koo to get us to take ourselves less seriously.

One of my (many) comedies of errors was no tragedy in the greater scheme of things. After an intense week of travel and moving our daughter into her new college dormitory, my husband and I stayed at a nice bed-and-breakfast—mostly just recovering. We were looking forward to spending a week of rest and relaxation in the Colorado Rockies.

On the first day of this much anticipated vacation, my beloved digital camera (with all the photos of our trip so far) went poof. Vanished in the chaos of the week.

After searching everywhere, it occurred to me that I might have left the camera on top of the car.

On foot patrol to retrace our drive the next day, I must have looked like a madwoman, scanning sidewalks and gutters of a busy street—sprinting so as not to get hit by cars . . . and a big rainstorm was coming my way.

Then it happened—a one-two punch: a twisted ankle and a torrential downpour of monsoon proportions, in that order.

Soaking wet, I hobbled back to the car and my waiting husband, who himself was ailing from a massive cold. Without missing a beat he says: "I'm just so glad we have a mountain view because that is just about as close to the mountains as we're going to get."

What else is there to do but laugh at the absurdity of our situation . . . then let go.

Shortly after the camera debacle, my sister happened to post this message on Facebook. Another koochie-koo from the big U: Tragedy + Time = Comedy.

LAUGH . . . *OUT LOUD*

Besides setting boundaries, self-care includes a healthy dose of humor. If you're not laughing every day, it's time to start. Laughter creates powerful chemicals in the brain that act quickly to reduce stress and tension and lower blood pressure. Lightening up your attitude will open new channels and new possibilities for change. It will immediately raise the energy in your home and life and make you feel more alive. The more joy you feel, the more you will radiate lightness and attract lighter people. Joy and laughter are the best beauty treatment I can think of.

I threw a birthday party for myself years ago to which I invited only those friends who would be fun and lively and appreciate Mexican food (my favorite). Instead of presents, I asked my friends to offer me a gift of their humor: I asked them to do something that would make me laugh.

Our next-door neighbor offered his tiny basement theater (yes, believe it or not, equipped with a little stage and a state-of-the-art lighting and sound system) for my friends to completely let loose and be the hams they really are. My funniest friend volunteered to act as master of ceremonies and was as good as or better than Leno and Letterman. People rose to the occasion and, one after the other, outdid themselves. The result was delightful, no holds barred, spontaneous, hysterical, magic! I laughed so hard my stomach muscles hurt for days afterward. I still look at the video we made of the event and am able to recapture the energy and joy of that moment. It remains one of the most unforgettable experiences of my life.

If you want to support yourself in feeling lighter, start laughing. Laugh with your spouse at the fact that your infant daughter threw up on you twice. Laugh at the fact that your car has broken down for the fifth time. Laugh at the fact that life seems to be giving you one lemon after another.

If you can't laugh, try one of those fake "ha ha" laughs a few times, and see what happens. As we learned in part 2, "acting as if" is no different from the real thing to the unconscious mind.

CLEARING PRACTICE
LIGHTENING UP

Do one thing that makes you laugh out loud, guffaw, split a seam—whatever it takes. If you need a little assist, try one of these suggestions.

◊ **Choose** to spend more time with people in your life who make you laugh a lot. Stay away from Debbie Downers.

◊ **Watch** reruns of funny shows, such as *I Love Lucy* or *Friends*. Tape them for later or when you really need a boost.

◊ **Google** "YouTube + Really Funny Videos."

◊ **Check out** the video clip in which Ellen DeGeneres talks on the phone to a ninety-year-old woman from Austin, Texas, named Gladys. "Ellen talks to Gladys Hardy + I love Jesus but I drink a little," is probably one of the funniest six minutes on YouTube that I have ever seen.

CLEARING JOURNAL

Use this space to recall and tap into the feeling of complete and utter joy.

◊ Some of the ways I have the most fun in my life are _____

◊ The people in my life who make me laugh (out loud) the most are _____

◊ The idea of being filled with joy all the time makes me feel

_____

◊ One thing I can do right now [today] that will lift my spirits is _____

Compassion

44 FORGIVE

Forgiveness is the fragrance that the violet sheds
on the heel that has crushed it.
—Mark Twain

How does one reconcile the loss of a loved one? How does one justify the premature death of a child or the untimely death of a parent, sibling, friend, or pet? How does one wrap one's brain around the 9-11 insanity, the slaughter of innocent animals, the decimation of an entire ethnic group, the inexplicable horrors that come from natural disasters and human error?

How does one forgive God, the universe, or whoever you want to blame for giving you an unsupportive spouse, an absentee parent, a hateful boss, an incompetent doctor, an unkind neighbor?

The answer, from a humanly attached place, is: not easily.

To have a heart so big that it can hold this much unbearable pain is advanced-level work.

CLEARING IS FORGIVING

I wanted to end this part on compassion with a chapter on forgiveness, because when all is said and done, compassion *is* forgiveness. To be truly clear and embody the best of who we are, we must let go. To let go—and *move on*—we must forgive.

So how do we do that advanced-level work, you might ask?

In a way, every single chapter in this book has been building your heart muscle. Clearing one baby step at a time is a practice in forgiveness. So too is compassionate self-care and your ability to detach and be "bigger than" the pain, the drama, and the stories. As bestselling author Debbie Ford says in her film *The Shadow Effect,* "Forgiveness doesn't happen in your head until it happens in your heart."

Where we humans often get tripped up is in believing that forgiveness means letting someone or some awful event off the hook. Not so says Marianne Williamson:

> The universe will deal with that person's Karma. You don't have to worry that if you "forgive them" that they're going to somehow live a deserved wonderful life. . . . It is not just to make their day better, it's to free *you.*

Give it up to God. Turn it over to a higher power. You do not have to carry the pain any more—either for yourself or the world. Let Divine Intelligence take care of it for you.

Clearing whatever you can handle and adopting lots of self-care are all you need to expand your heart space. You never know; it could lead you to revelations beyond your wildest imaginings.

So, from what slight, hurt, or insult do you wish to free yourself? For what, or whom, would you like to hold a space today? Whom would you like to forgive?

Consider it handled.

CLEARING PRACTICE
FORGIVING

Here is an opportunity to practice forgiving someone (or something) *and* yourself using the prompts below to guide you.

1. **Someone or Something:** Release attachment to your need for justice and just let . . . it . . . go.

2. **Yourself:** Let go of attachment to your need for things to turn out the way you had planned.

Keep practicing every day and notice the changes—in you.

CLEARING JOURNAL

Take as long as you need to reflect on what it means to forgive and let go completely of attachment. Use the prompts below or go off road—whatever helps you dig deep and tell the truth.

- ◊ Someone [something] I am ready to forgive now is _____ (what gets in my way is _____)

- ◊ When I think about opening my heart and letting [this unconscionable act, shameful situation, horrible person, myself] "off the hook," I feel _____

- ◊ When I consider surrendering my pain to a higher power, I feel _____

- ◊ Some of the shifts [changes, dreams] that I'm noticing since I began this journey in clearing are _____

COMPASSION

Joy naturally springs from being spacious. It is the best beauty treatment.

The energy of spaciousness is our birthright: It is free, portable, attractive, and magnetic.

Clearing with compassion is holding a space for ourselves.

Self-care is the softening balm of clearing.

Good sleep and regular nap taking repairs and restores the body, promotes expanded states of consciousness, and feeds the soul.

Drinking water—half our body weight in ounces per day—promotes health and balance.

Eating real food (that you can cook and pronounce) is nourishing and clearing, too.

It is easier to let go when we feel supported—physically and emotionally.

Rubbing on or soaking in a mixture of sea salt, baking soda, and water helps to minimize stress and integrates the energetic side effects of clutter clearing.

Humans are hardwired for cooperation and compassion.

Laughter is a surefire way to raise the energy in our home and life; it reduces stress and tension.

Letting go is forgiveness at its core.

Forgiveness is clearing.

PART VI

WISDOM
REVEAL THY TRUE SELF

I have allowed myself the freedom and flexibility
to declutter my spaces, internal and external,
at a pace that works for me, be it one minute or one hour.
I am working on a project towards performance poetry.
I am turning 69 this year. The artist within
has awakened from a deep long sleep
to express herself and to celebrate!
The phoenix rises out of the debris of the past.
—letter from "a happy declutterer"

45 CLEARING WITH WISDOM

Then comes a moment of feeling
the wings you've grown, lifting.
—**Rumi**

Have you ever spent any time taking nothing personally or even seriously?
Yes, doing nothing more than observing your thoughts and not attaching any
importance to any of them?

A few years ago, my husband and I treated ourselves to an experience of
doing just that. We took two weeks off and went on a meditation retreat on a
spectacular Greek island. For practiced meditators like my husband, "a treat"
would be the fitting description. For me at the time, a relative newbie to these
long-term marathons in mindfulness, it would be more accurate to call the
experience "being-with-a-mind-that-won't-shut-up" or, depending on the day
you asked me, just *plain hell.*

Ours was not your typical ascetic experience where you sit like a pretzel for
hours on end. It was a deluxe variation held at a beautiful resort with sweeping
views of the Aegean. Every day was a feast of seventy-degree weather, gourmet
vegetarian dinners, fun-loving participants, inspiring teachers, soul-feeding lessons in human consciousness. Two whole weeks where we were given permission
(instructed, actually) to do absolutely nothing . . . and take nothing seriously.

Heaven, you might say, were it not for the all-consuming orgy of thinking
spewing in my head; a gluttonous rehashing of self-importance, *poor me,* and

nonstop *woulda-coulda-shouldas*—all of which I found utterly exhausting, nauseating, and even physically painful. The fact that I happened to be on one of the most beautiful places on the planet was completely lost on me.

So why do something in paradise that is so *not* pleasing? I asked myself this question countless times while I thrashed about like an addict in rehab, ready to bolt at any minute. The answer: week two.

Disarming the monkey mind and unwinding from "very important" thought bulletins, such as *"I need a cup of coffee . . . Caffeine is bad . . . My back hurts . . . I hate this . . . I love this . . . I signed up for this?! . . . Thirteen-and-a-half days to go . . . Everyone is 'getting this' but me . . . My back hurts . . ."* takes time.

And massive doses of compassionate self-care.

It's not the thoughts themselves, I would later discover, but the constant *chewing* (identifying, personalizing, feeding, attaching) of them that can be so tiresome. Stop the chewing, and the relief is instantaneous. Like the relief you feel in your mouth when you finally remember to spit out the tasteless wad of gum.

Though the mind has no concept of this (and never will)—and employs a spectacular array of stealth tactics to charm us back into our old habits—the alternative to a grasping way of life is pretty darn sweet. It's the magic that happens when we choose ease. Or take nothing personally. Or surrender to that deep silent space within us that simply *knows.*

By the end of my second week of mindful non-doing, something began to poke through the noise and clutter of my mind. Nothing fancy or earth shattering, really. No fireworks or big revelations.

What came into focus was *me.* Like those three-dimensional pictures that come into focus when you soften your gaze: It's the "me" that has been there all along. The me who hangs out in that timeless space where everything feels uncomplicated and clear.

Living in present time. Now *that* is what I would call paradise!

The gateway to infinite wisdom.

NEW *YOU* COMING THROUGH

What makes this journey so interesting and fun are the wondrous "reveals" that come out of adopting a regular daily clearing practice. As the Buddha said, "What you are is what you have been; what you will be is what you do now."

There is no telling what will emerge as a result of shedding all those skins of your former self. That is for you to discover as you continue on the clearing path. As the real—bigger—you emerges from behind the veil of stress and stuff, it is likely that you will find yourself feeling and doing things you never felt or did before. Expanding into your natural state of being spacious—one moment, step, thought, or drawer at a time—has a magical way of making you feel more available and in the flow, as if life were living you instead of you living it.

You may experience the ordinary with new eyes and insight, as one student shares here:

> I've had a real insight today. I realize that I do not pay attention when I put things away. I psychologically detach myself from this obnoxious business which wastes my time when I could be doing something else more interesting. To my surprise, when I focus my awareness on placing an object carefully in its home, I get pleasure from that. Applying awareness to what I am doing, yes, even if it is clearing up—boring clearing up—gives me pleasure. How amazing!

You may notice that you don't worry as much about the future or what people think as you did before, and your buttons don't get pressed as often by people and events in your life. You may notice that as your attachments begin to lose their charge, your physical clutter becomes less of an issue and, through effortless clearing, simply falls away.

You may experience your body—as I often do when I'm in my "spacious zone"—gliding gracefully through the day, free of friction or resistance, like that feeling you get when you're sitting in one of those glider rocking chairs. You may experience physical changes, such as greater ease in movement, a loss of excess weight, a clarity in your eyesight, a softening of your skin . . . yes, even a clearing of your sinuses!

*Your
Spacious
Self*

You may observe longer stretches of quiet stillness between your thoughts or profound openings of inspiration or a deep inner knowing that simply takes your breath away. You may notice that the world itself seems more sparkly and alive to you, revealing its divine mystery in tiny details you had never noticed before. Trees shine, people smile, miracles happen. Guess what? This is the world mirroring *you* back to you! Enjoy it. It is just the beginning!

In this last part, I offer my best practices, favorite tools, and secrets that you can use to build a clearing "way of life" that is both sustaining and sustainable. These resources will give you a means to play with, integrate, and deepen your experience of the material in this book for years to come.

46 SHIFT HAPPENS

Change happens slowly, then all at once.
—Jay W. Vogt

GROWING PAINS

Clearing can be strange and inscrutable sometimes. You can be humming along in your life, feeling supremely spacious, and suddenly out of nowhere find yourself flattened by an emotional squall or physical unpleasantness that you never saw coming.

In my earlier years of clearing out a drawer or a bookcase, for example, I would notice my body feeling inordinately tired, gummy, sluggish, and congested (as if I'd just entered a smoke-filled room). My feet would often ache, my breathing would become shallow, and I'd be massively thirsty. On some days, I'd even wake up feeling like I'd been hit by a sledgehammer, incapable of moving my neck more than an inch in either direction. *What the heck is this!? Just yesterday I was feeling like a million bucks!*

Though each person responds differently to clearing, it is not uncommon sometimes to feel worse—or "less clear"—than when you started. Before chanting, "This-is-not-*wor*-king!" you might want to consider what I tell my clients and students: Clearing stress patterns lifts the lid on the more deeply held issues that *you couldn't even feel before.*

The fact that you are feeling bad or gummy or congested or immobilized means that you are feeling something! You are feeling areas in your being that you've never allowed yourself to feel in the past. This is good. It means that you are waking up!

Have you ever held a tight fist for a long period of time and noticed that it becomes numb after a while, then you don't notice it anymore? When you begin to relax your fist, you might not notice much at first, then the hand hurts! Clearing physical, mental, and emotional clutter is like that. What you may experience as weather are the pins and needles of waking up after holding on for an entire lifetime. Your job now is to be as gentle with yourself as you can. Remember that feeling "good/bad/whatever"—without attachment—*is clearing!*

SIGNPOSTS OF CLUTTER CLEARING

That said, it is no comfort to know that there may be some unexpected bumps lurking ahead. It is natural human behavior to seek instant gratification for our efforts. Our hope is to feel lighter after a few hours or a weekend wrangling our stuff into boxes and trash bags or after sitting on a cushion in lotus position. But because most of us are looking at a lifetime of holding patterns, it can take some time for the "softening tools" to produce their desired effect. Revealing deeply held attachments can bring up even more weather and throw us off course if we're not paying attention.

When you clear using the exercises in this book, you put into motion some powerful intentions. No matter how minuscule your clearing efforts and goals may seem, it's important to remember that clearing, even just one toothpick or one hairball—with awareness—will create an opening into spaciousness.

The four markers described below will help you recognize some of the natural phases that can spring up as a result of a daily practice in clearing. They'll help you recognize that something might, in fact, be shifting for you, even if the changes are too subtle to notice or the outcomes are not exactly what you were expecting.

Here are the signposts; think of them as little "weather advisories" to carry on the road with you.

1. Feelings come up—*allow* them.

2. Shift happens—*embrace* it.

3. Outcomes change—*accept* them.

4. Clarity comes into focus—*trust* it.

Here's what they mean.

FEELINGS COME UP—ALLOW THEM

By definition, clutter clearing releases energy that has been stuck for a long time, sometimes for an entire lifetime. When energy is moved in a big way, it is possible to feel more tired than usual or more cranky and edgy or uncomfortable. You may feel more emotional or have a bout of panic or grief, anger or sadness. You may notice yourself shutting down completely. You may experience spaciness, memory lapses, or mental fog; you may feel the opposite, more alive, energized, excited, and clear.

You may yawn more than usual or tear up or burp or fart or feel nauseated. You may get unexplainable physical symptoms like headaches or backaches. You may sleep more, or you may have too much energy to sleep. You may want to quit. You may feel more out of control or desperate to escape and have cravings for food, alcohol, TV, exercise. You may feel awesome one moment and completely fall apart the next—all in less than sixty seconds!

Symptoms of clearing are the myriad ways that the body processes old stuff that is coming to the surface. They are signs of detoxification that result from raising the energetic frequencies in our home and in our life. They are ways the ego copes with the idea of letting go and feeling "those feelings." They are the result of expansion energies colliding with contraction energies—no different from a high-pressure system slamming into your sluggish low-pressure holding patterns. Storms come up naturally. Don't be too hard on yourself.

SHIFT HAPPENS—EMBRACE IT

One of my favorite quotes is by Ram Dass, who acknowledges what happens to us when our tightly held self-concept begins to break apart: "There is a grief that occurs when who you thought you were starts to disappear." To those of you who feel that your very identity is deconstructing before your own eyes, take comfort and allow yourself to feel this loss. Letting go of heavy-duty holding patterns can feel like a death. Honor these phases, for it *is* a true dying of your former self as it makes room for something new.

Shifts can come in other forms, too. One stage in childbirth is called transition. This is when the mother is shifting from labor to pushing mode. It is typically the shortest and the most intense stage of the entire birth and is a signpost that the end of labor is near.

There are transition points in clearing, too, that take us to whole new levels of awareness within ourselves. There's no mistaking these. These are the times when clearing your clutter might result in a healing crisis or a crisis of confidence. You might lose your job or home or your partner of twenty-five years. You may feel totally alone or empty or disconnected from your life purpose. You may find yourself at the end of your rope, ready to throw in the towel, shouting obscenities at anything that moves. As George Leonard says: "Your resistance to change is likely to reach its peak when significant change is imminent." Pay close attention to this marker. It may be a clue that something is about to shift for you in what could be a very *big* and positive way.

In the clearing journey, the universe has a way of giving us what we need but not always what we want. If any of the big storms do try to knock you down, don't lose heart, and don't give up. Remember, it is the nature of this stage to *not know.* Give yourself a lot of supporting self-care, and trust that you will get through it. It is precisely at this stage that your holding patterns are losing their grip on you. You're about to see a whole other side to your being that's been hanging out there all along. No matter how bad it feels, I'm here to tell you: This is a very good sign. Congratulations!

OUTCOMES CHANGE—ACCEPT THEM

You might also attract what I like to call freebies from the universe. Freebies are those divine nuisances that we get at the most inopportune moments.

Usually unsolicited, they remind us to pay attention. They give us new opportunities to shift our perception and reframe our thoughts.

Delays in traffic, cancelled flights, computer crashes. These freebies are a much subtler version of a healing crisis. Freebies often give us a clue that something we're doing is off, and we're being nudged back on. Freebies can also be an indicator of something being very *right* for once. Not getting into the supposed "best" college or losing the bid on a particular job or house you wanted may be a blessing in disguise.

You can ask the universe to bring these freebies on gently, in ways that you will understand and easily integrate into your life. Use them to practice letting go. They are great teachers.

CLARITY COMES INTO FOCUS—TRUST IT

As you clear away the clutter of your life, you become more aware of information coming through that feels true and right. This is powerful because, in fact, it is pure, uncontaminated, and unfiltered information that is bypassing the rational, ego-driven monkey mind. You may not be able to explain what is coming through, but some part of you just *knows*. Don't dismiss those little flutters of clarity. Don't deny those true feelings of inspiration that have a way of sneaking in the back door. It will seem as if your radio signals are coming through with much less static. You will see things you haven't seen before, and the world may look more vibrant and alive to you.

Information may show up as an intuition to do or not do something. It may show up as a dream, an opportunity, a phone call, or a synchronicity. If you pay close attention, you may notice that what's bubbling up are the stirrings of your soul, your highest wisdom—your true, most spacious self. Embrace and enjoy these moments. They are just the beginning.

CLEARING PRACTICE
WONDERING

The practice consists of asking yourself wonder questions. [*Psst,* "wonder questions" are not meant to be answered but stepped into, mused . . . *lived.*]

◊ What is my soul here to do?

◊ What am I birthing?

◊ What needs to be cleared for this to happen?

Use your journal to explore these questions more deeply.

CLEARING JOURNAL

Take a moment to reflect on some of your deepest yearnings and some of the shifts that are taking place in your life since you began clearing.

◊ I believe that I am on this planet to _____

◊ I know this is true because _____

◊ I am making space for the emerging me by _____

◊ I recognize some of the bumps in my life as growing pains because _____

◊ I can tell some shifts are taking place already because _____

47 MAKE A PLAN

Tell me, what is it you plan to do
with your one wild and precious life?
—**Mary Oliver**

As we have learned and practiced, the essence of clearing in this book boils
down to our ability to:

◊ allow, not judge

◊ respond, not react

◊ be more, do less

What makes this possible are the four guiding principles for clearing in this
book: Intention, Action, Non-identification, and Compassion.

Think of these as equal members of your clearing team that will give you
the best possible results. You couldn't do this work effectively without any of
them. Consider that action without intention has no rudder, no direction, no
purpose. Similarly, intention without action yields only untapped potential.
Take away non-identification, and you're left with dangling emotional attachments, lots of drama, and a heavy heart. Without compassion, you're unable to
get past the machinations of the "toddler" mind; to feel safe, supported, in the
flow, and bigger than your clutter. It is worth noting that action, which is the
driving force behind most traditional approaches to clearing and organizing in
our culture, comprises only one fourth of the clearing work!

Though each principle has been introduced separately in this book and can by itself make a huge difference in clearing your clutter, it isn't until all four are applied and practiced as a *unified whole* that the real magic occurs. It is the confluence of these four energy streams that creates a powerful force for change.

To build an effective practice of clearing, we need consistency. In my book, consistency means *daily*. Adopting a daily practice, no matter how small the task or effort, will soften holding patterns and release the buildup of stress and weather over time.

Therefore, my prescription for a lasting clearing program is to choose at least one offering from each of the four guiding principles every day. Neglecting one of these pathways would be like taking a leg off a table. The program loses its strength and stability and diminishes the return for effort.

Any time a task feels overwhelming, the secret is to cut back your daily practice by reducing and repeating *all four* elements. Taking the gentler R&R approach means that you reduce a clearing task, perimeter, or time spent on a task to a range that feels manageable, and you repeat the action until the task is complete or no longer elicits resistance.

THE BASIC FOUR

Here they are—your keys to the kingdom of living clear:

1. **Intention:** Reframe belief patterns, anchor intentions, and quiet the mind with the Softening Attitudes (sets 1–4) and the Attitudes of Gratitude with your eyes closed from one to twenty minutes, at least once a day. Practice with your eyes open anytime you think of them.

2. **Action:** Sweep, move, put away, round up, clean, clear, or address *one* thing, pile, area, toleration, and/or issue, every day. Keep tasks small enough to bypass the fear response.

3. **Non-identification:** Mind your "shoulds." Observe and allow weather patterns by reframing "I" statements with "This is . . ." anytime you think of it. Additionally or alternately, repeat silently, "It's not mine," "Strike that," or "Don't go there" anytime you feel your buttons getting

pressed. Stop and feel often throughout the day—without attachment—to release charge. [*Psst,* I recommend revisiting Clearing Is Feeling in chapter 7 if the concept of feeling with detachment continues to elude you.]

4. **Compassion:** Create a feeling of safety and joy every day by doing at least one thing that activates your senses, makes your heart sing, is fun, and *feels good.* Practice the Floor Pose every day. Lighten up with laughter.

SUGGESTED WEEKLY PRACTICE

The four basic tools described above provide an excellent base for creating a weekly clearing plan that is easy and adaptable to your needs. The Clearing Plan Worksheet in appendix 1 will give you a place to clarify your intentions, write down your goals, track your progress, and hold yourself accountable. You won't need this weekly practice tool after your clearing becomes a natural way of life.

Here's how to use the worksheet to create an ongoing clearing practice for yourself:

1. **Begin:** Photocopy a weekly worksheet from the two-page template provided in appendix 1. If you would like to continue past one week, which I highly recommend, photocopy six double-sided sheets—enough for a six-week period.

2. **Make a Plan:** Choose one day (preferably the same day) each week to fill out your worksheet. Create a plan that is realistic and doable (*read:* a bit of a stretch but not overwhelming).

3. **Check Off:** Mark the tasks after you have completed them each day in the chart at the bottom of the worksheet.

4. **Review:** At the end of the week, review your progress and fine-tune your intentions for the upcoming week should you choose to continue.

5. **Renew:** Give yourself a fresh start each week by filling in a

new worksheet, even if you have not completed all the tasks of the previous week.

6. **Praise:** Always praise your efforts, no matter how small they may feel. Remember that judging yourself for lack of progress only adds more clutter to your clutter!

7. **Optional:** The worksheet can also be used to establish and discuss goals with others in your Clearing Circle support group [described later in this part].

STAY TRUE

This little memory aid will help you clear a path to your TRUE nature. Post it on your mirror, dashboard, fridge, or desktop. Use it as a gentle reminder to incorporate the Basic Four into your daily practice. It will serve you well, especially if the Suggested Weekly Practice described above is still too much to manage and wrap your monkey mind around.

◊ **T**—*Thank:* Express gratitude.

◊ **R**—*Reduce and Repeat:* Reduce to one task (area of focus or time spent) and repeat until the task is complete or time is up.

◊ **U**—*Unplug:* Detach by reframing one "I" statement with "This is . . ."

◊ **E**—*Elevate:* Do something that lifts your spirits and feels good.

CLEARING PRACTICE
CREATING A GAME PLAN

Make a clearing plan for the week using the Suggested Weekly Practice as your base. Use your clearing journal or a photocopy of the worksheet located in appendix 1.

CLEARING JOURNAL

Use your journal time to tune in to any resistance that may arise as a result of creating a game plan for yourself and/or completing the tasks at hand.

◊ What I am finding most soothing about making a plan is
_____

◊ What is pushing my buttons about making a plan is _____

◊ It is easy for me to follow through on my goals because [*psst*, name and feel the part of you that is rebelling and believes that it is *not easy*] _____

◊ It is easy for me to dial it down when I get overwhelmed because _____

◊ What I have already accomplished since I began setting doable tasks is [*psst*, name and feel the part of you that believes that it is still not enough] _____

FINE-TUNE

48

You want beautiful? Watch the steam
undulating and swirling off a cup of coffee,
illuminated by sunlight streaming through a window.
—Amy Hillman, on Twitter

All our window shades needed replacing in the living room. The resulting effect of a temporary half-curtain treatment has been a stunning revelation. What I see are none of the usual cars, or houses, or people walking by.

Just the tops of everything. Nothing to see from my usual sofa perch but an explosion of trees in springtime!

This "new" view has been mesmerizing. I see trees in the distance that I had never noticed before. Trees up close, like our crabapple waiting for the first warm day to finally pop. Overlays of moving green and copper and pink and red.

Thanks to the wee bit of sky poking through the branches, I can see that the trees are dancing! It's a breathtaking party going on out there.

What is one thing of beauty staring you right in the face? Something that has always been there—something you have not noticed before.

Place your attention on that.

FINE-TUNE

As we have seen already, this book presents four sets of phrases that are designed to invite simplicity and quiet the mind. Each comes with its own companion simple meditation.

Here they are again. They make a gorgeous bouquet when they appear together, don't they?

Set 1	Set 2	Set 3	Set 4
I am enough	I choose ease	I am here	I rest in stillness
I have enough	I choose peace	I am now	I rest in awareness
There is enough	I choose joy	I accept	I rest
		I allow	

They are quite versatile, as well. Besides the daily recommended practices, you can also apply any of the phrase sequences to address a specific issue or circumstance that is weighing you down.

Here are some examples of new ways to play:

1. **Attached:** If you are clearing a closet of sentimental attachments or taking a box over to the consignment shop, set 1 ("I am enough," "I have enough," "There is enough") might help you soften your attachment and let them go.

2. **Overwhelmed:** If you are feeling harried, rushed, or overwhelmed, you might reach for set 2 ("I choose ease," "I choose peace," "I choose joy") or simply use "I choose ease" by itself.

3. **Impatient:** If you are stuck in traffic, waiting in line or for a plane that is delayed, or anxiously waiting for a diagnosis from your doctor, you might choose set 3 ("I am here," "I am now," "I accept," "I allow"). Be sure to breathe.

4. **Stuck:** Set 4 ("I rest in stillness," "I rest in awareness," "I rest") is especially wonderful when you are practicing yoga

or tai chi, taking a walk in the woods, or having trouble falling asleep. You could practice this set to clear the channels for added inspiration in writing, music, art.

If none of the phrases fit your current situation or inspire you, perhaps this instruction from the famous nineteenth-century philosopher Ralph Waldo Emerson might help you to uncover your personal mantra:

> There is guidance for each of us, and by lowly listening we shall hear the right word. . . . Place yourself in the middle of the stream of power and wisdom which [flows into your life], and you are without effort impelled to truth . . . and a perfect contentment.

There are infinite ways to fine-tune your clearing practice. Every moment is a new one. If something isn't working for you on this journey, change the channel. Place your focus on something that *does* lift your spirits and lighten your load.

CLEARING PRACTICE
FINE-TUNING

Start by softening your gaze and allowing your heart to guide you toward one word, phrase, or set of phrases from any of the four lists above or one of your own. Notice what happens when you simply place yourself in the flow of a word or phrase and allow yourself to be moved by it. Where does it take you? How does it feel?

If none of them speak to you, close your eyes and wait until something reveals itself to you.

Next, try the directed meditation described below, especially if you are feeling stuck, and watch what happens.

DIRECTED SIMPLE MEDITATION
1. **Begin** by first getting in touch with the weather you are feeling. Perhaps it's a problem you can't seem to resolve or a grudge you can't seem to shake or a feeling of stress and exhaustion that results from something you have no control over, such as staying up all night with a sick child or putting up with noisy neighbors or street chaos.

2. **Choose** a set of Attitudes that best fit the circumstance, and practice repeating the set with your eyes closed for five to twenty minutes or with your eyes open anytime you remember.

3. **Notice** how you feel afterward. Notice your body, thoughts, and any additional weather that comes up.

4. **Fine-tune.** Is the charge you were holding as strong as it was before? Did you receive any insight you didn't previously have?

CLEARING JOURNAL

Take a moment in your journal to reflect on what it feels like to see something new in your life and how fine-tuning your clearing practice changes your experience.

◊ A thing of beauty staring right at me right now (that I hadn't noticed before) is _____

◊ When I place my attention on beauty, I feel _____

◊ Before the directed meditation, I was feeling _____ (and afterwards _____)

◊ Some of the ways that I can cultivate more simplicity and beauty in my life are _____

◊ The difference for me between "looking" and "seeing" is _____

JOIN WITH OTHERS 49

You cannot grow yourself by yourself.
—Katherine Woodward Thomas and Claire Zammit

TALKING ABOUT CLEARING . . . *IS* CLEARING

Circles, by definition, hold a space. They're nonlinear. They're mysterious. They're generative. Add open-minded individuals who are willing to be present and not attached to a particular outcome, and the circle becomes a safe and transformative vehicle for clearing clutter.

This is the design of my listening groups—women mostly—who come together once a week for six weeks to share their triumphs and challenges with clutter clearing. Sometimes our gatherings generate a lot of animated stories, relief, and laughter. Sometimes our discussions reveal deeper emotional weather patterns that sound something like this:

◊ I've lost my sense of myself.

◊ Clutter in my body, in the hours, the schedules . . .

◊ I find myself clearing out my son's bookcase, or my daughter's, and avoiding my own.

◊ The phrase "I choose ease" makes my skin crawl.

◊ I'm so envious of people who are able to get things done.

◊ There's a loud voice in me saying *Let me out!*

And sometimes we just sit in silence and wait for something to happen—just observing what *that* feels like.

No matter what arises, one thing is almost always certain: We often walk away feeling lighter without having lifted a finger to clear at home! After all these years in the clearing trenches, I can say without a doubt that joining together with other compassionate souls increases the visible and invisible layers you are likely to shed, *exponentially.*

WITNESSING IS CLEARING

The thing that sets the clearing circle format apart from the solo approach to clearing clutter is the effect of the witnessing process to release holding patterns. It is the safe container of the circle that invites and allows anything to be said and held without judgment. None of it needs to add up or make sense for it to be worthy and powerful. As long as the simple ground rules are observed (e.g., "We are not here to fix anything or anyone," "Everything we share stays here," and so on), anything goes.

Participants find that their pain or shame, their fear or loneliness is not unique to them. They see that everyone has their own special brand of holding on: their own embarrassing stories, messy foibles and dramas, silly quirks, dark secrets. These profound realizations help everyone come out of the closet, laugh more, and move forward into that magical spaciousness that surfaces naturally when we speak our truth.

If this sounds really cool, it's because *it is!* And it costs nothing to try. If you already belong to a book group or support group, consider taking a six-week (or six-month) side trip. Or ask one or more of your friends with whom you feel most comfortable if they'd be interested in joining you on a clearing adventure.

Set a date and a time, agree on a venue, and allow about two hours for your gatherings. Most importantly, have fun!

CREATE YOUR OWN CLEARING CIRCLE

Whom can you think of in your life who might like to join you in some clearing, slowing down, and simplifying? Are you already a member of a book group, women's circle, church group, gardening club, sewing circle, poker night, . . . whatever? I am sure there are others in your life who might really enjoy going on a ride with you—even if it is *just one* other person who lives halfway around the world! With Internet phones and Skype available now, it doesn't matter where people live.

Starting a clearing support group is easy, too: All the steps you need to create and maintain a circle of your own, and six sample meeting agendas, are neatly outlined in appendices 2 and 3. The guidelines are easy to modify to suit any group size or timetable.

What do you say? If any of this sounds intriguing, give it a try. You may be pleasantly surprised.

CLEARING PRACTICE
PARTNERING

Make a list of one to five people with whom you could imagine forming a clearing circle. Use the steps outlined in the appendices to get you started. Notice any resistance you have to putting yourself out there.

CLEARING JOURNAL

Use this space to brainstorm clearing circle possibilities and any resistance behaviors and fears that get in your way.

◊ People [friends, co-workers, family members] with whom I feel most safe and who might be interested in partnering with me are _____

◊ It is easy and safe for me to declare that I want to start a group because [*psst,* notice the fears and name them] _____

◊ Joining with others will take my clearing to a whole new level because [*psst,* notice your resistance, where it shows up in your body, and name it] _____

◊ My deepest yearning is _____

50 TAKE STOCK

The purpose of life is to unlearn what has been learned, and to remember what has been forgotten.
—Sufi saying

So . . . how's it going?

There are the obvious external clues of clearing success, of course: an emptier bookcase, more white space in your email inbox, a new love interest, a job offer. But what about the internal markers? How spacious and detached and present can you truly be when the next family reunion rolls around? Or a child becomes seriously ill? Are you able to glide about your life without so much as a button getting pressed?

Clearing has a strange effect on us humans. When we let go of attachments to things and outcomes, and our buttons don't get pressed as much, we *forget that we even had them!* It may be hard to believe, but it's true.

What is one shift or positive change you've experienced in your home or life since you began reading this book? If you can't think of anything, perhaps the questions below will jiggle loose some awareness.

◊ Are you feeling lighter? Calmer?

◊ Do you notice yourself clearing, or having the urge to clear and put away more often?

◊ Does your home or apartment feel bigger? Smaller? Different?

- ◊ Is there an opportunity or a relationship that you have attracted in the past month (positive or negative)?

- ◊ Have you noticed any changes in your health, sleep patterns, eating patterns?

- ◊ Have you noticed any changes in your relationship with a family member?

- ◊ Are you aware of an increased or decreased sense of smell (taste, touch, sight, hearing, intuition)?

- ◊ Are you able to become more of a witness to the emotional weather instead of *being* the weather?

- ◊ Are you laughing more, having fun, feeling in the flow?

- ◊ Have you experienced any interesting synchronicities, dreams, shifts in perception, revelations?

Without judging any shifts as "good" or "bad," remember that in the greater scheme, clearing anything, big or small, is about opening the channels to that place within that is uncomplicated and unplugged, sparkly and clear. While the ego is concerned with our comfort, the soul doesn't care if we're comfortable or not. Its sole (soul) purpose is to help us evolve.

CLEARING PRACTICE
TAKING STOCK

The practice is to reflect on the shifts you have experienced in your journey so far.

CLEARING JOURNAL

As you write in your journal, consider setting some clear intentions and goals that you'd like to make toward becoming a more clear and spacious you.

- ◊ Some of the shifts and glimmers of clarity that I've experienced since I began clearing in earnest have been _____

- ◊ Some of the pleasant and not-so-pleasant outcomes that I've encountered on this ride, and how I handled them, include _____

◊ Other shifts, dreams, synchronicities, *ah-has* that I have experienced are _____

◊ My biggest take-away or *ah-ha* has been _____

◊ My goals from this day forward are to _____

THINK BIG

51

Remember, the entrance door to the sanctuary is inside you.
—Rumi

What can I say. I'm a teacher. I love making sense of things in the shortest, simplest ways. If it helps you see where we've been and where we are going with all this clearing business, have a look at the chart below. It's called A Paradigm Shift in Clutter Clearing.

How does the right-hand column compare to your worldview?

More importantly, how does it make you feel?

A Paradigm Shift in Clutter Clearing

Clutter and Clearing: The Old View	Clutter and Clearing: A New View
1. Clutter is solid matter: physical and visible.	1. Clutter is stuck energy that manifests first as thought, word, and deed.
2. Clutter is separate from us.	2. Clutter is an extension of us.
3. Clutter grows like a weed.	3. Clutter grows as a result of human unawareness.

4. Clutter is bad, a nuisance, something to be ashamed of.	4. Clutter is a teacher; it reflects the places in us that we have yet to love and heal.
5. Clearing is a linear process.	5. Clearing is a journey.
6. Clearing is pushing through resistance and "throwing away."	6. Clearing is softening resistance and "letting go."
7. Clearing is a mindless, tedious exercise.	7. Clearing is a mindful *practice*.
8. Clearing is about making a change.	8. Clearing is about *allowing* a change.
9. Clearing can be used to bury and deny our feelings.	9. Clearing can be used to allow and experience our feelings.
10. Clearing creates a pathway to our door.	10. Clearing creates a pathway to our most spacious self: the compassionate heart.

CLEARING PRACTICE
EXPANDING INTO SPACIOUSNESS

Take an index card and slowly move it down the chart above, revealing both columns of each line item at the same time. Notice which concepts and phrases resonate or pop the most for you, and which do not, by how you feel when you tune in.

CLEARING JOURNAL

Use this space to reflect on the ways that you have changed, or not.

◊ Some of the concepts from the chart that really resonate for me are _____

◊ Some of the concepts that continue to elude me [press my buttons, make my head spin] are _____

◊ Some of the ways that I feel I have changed since I started clearing are _____

Your Spacious Self

START OVER

52

> There will come a time when you believe
> everything is finished. That will be the beginning.
> —**Louis L'Amour**

Last New Year's Eve I posted this line on my Facebook page: "Every moment is a happy new year. Enjoy yours!"

Someone wrote in: "Kinda cool . . . new chance at starting over. I would love to get it right."

To which I replied: "The idea of getting it right suggests you're doing it wrong—a concept that doesn't exist when you're living in present time. I say stay with 'now' and you're golden. Happy starting over—and over—again!"

In spacious speak, the concept of wanting to get something right is simply the monkey mind piping in when it doesn't like something or is attached to something or is remembering something . . . *from the past*. The only thing that is real—and really juicy—is happening right now.

In case it hasn't dawned on you as we come to the final chapter in this book, here's a little news flash: The clearing journey never ends; it just gets better, juicier, and more fun!

Remember, consistency, not quantity, is the key to freedom and lasting change.

CLEARING PRACTICE
REMEMBERING

Read the part of this book called "An Ongoing Journey: Ten Truths and Ten Keys," located just after the summary points for part 6. Place an index card over both lists in the chart and reveal one line from the Ten Truths, one column at time.

Repeat with the list of Ten Keys.

Notice the line items with which you resonate the most and the ones that make you feel queasy.

Make friends with the queasy ones. They are your teachers.

CLEARING JOURNAL

Use this space to explore the "truths" and "keys" that you connected with and didn't. Use it to add your own list of truths and keys.

◊ I resonated most with these truths and keys _____ (because _____)

◊ The truths and keys that pressed my buttons the most were _____ (because _____)

◊ It is safe for me to believe that [insert a truth or key that you found objectionable from the lists; name and feel the weather that it elicits] because _____

◊ What I believe is true for me is _____

◊ What I believe is the key to my lasting success is _____

WISDOM

It is normal in clearing for there to be periods of expansion followed by periods of contraction.

Clearing stress patterns lifts the lid on the more deeply held issues that we couldn't even feel before. That is why they're called growing pains.

Feeling "good/bad/whatever"—with awareness and detachment—is clearing.

There are transition points in clearing that take us to whole new levels of awareness within ourselves.

Intention, Action, Non-identification, and Compassion are the four pathways to cultivating a clear home and a spacious life; clearing is sustainable only when all four principles are applied and practiced as a unified whole.

Talking about clearing, and listening with presence (witnessing), is clearing.

Clearing circles help reduce our individual and collective load—exponentially.

Consistency, not quantity, is the key to freedom and lasting change.

The clearing journey never ends; it just gets better, juicier, and more fun!

AN ONGOING JOURNEY:
TEN TRUTHS AND TEN KEYS

I decided to start anew, to strip away what I had been taught.
—**Georgia O'Keefe**

Because the nature of clearing is to continuously unfold, I invite you to revisit this book often. You will be a different person every time you read it. You may see something that didn't register before. You may notice that some of the exercises or journal contemplations that once eluded you make more sense to you now. Use this book to tweak and further your practice—to shed the kind of light that delivers those amazing moments that make it all worth it. Use it to guide and support you, even as you become more clear! Consider it a safe haven, a pathway to your true self.

That being said, it is good to remember that the practices and tools in this book are only a vehicle. They ultimately do not replace your deeper wisdom to know and act from your own truth. They do not replace your ability to feel what is alive and cooking for yourself. As Lao Tsu wrote back in 565 BC:

> Learn to unclutter your mind. Learn to simplify your work. As you rely less and less on knowing just what to do, your work will become more direct and more powerful. You will discover that the quality of your consciousness is more potent than any tech-

nique or theory or interpretation. Learn how fruitful the blocked group or individual suddenly becomes when you give up trying to do just the right thing.

Don't forget to have fun while you're at it!

I leave you with two summaries that offer ten truths about the clearing journey and ten keys to your lasting success. Copy and place them where you are likely to see them regularly, and allow them to illuminate your path.

Ten Truths about the Journey	Ten Keys to Lasting Success
1. Things change.	1. Keep it simple.
2. Things are not always what they seem.	2. Go slowly, but keep moving.
3. Some things cannot be understood with the rational mind.	3. Honor your limits, be gentle, and do only what feels right.
4. The body knows. Trust it.	4. Let go of attachment to the outcome.
5. Each moment is an opportunity to let go.	5. Be grateful all the time.
6. No task is too small.	6. Be a witness to your emotional weather: observe and listen, stop and feel.
7. Clearing clutter makes room for something new to come into our lives.	7. Notice, and note, what you are attracting—without attachment.
8. Clearing clutter sheds light on that which we have kept in the dark.	8. Invite wonder, not worry, into your life.
9. Spaciousness "in here" translates into spaciousness "out there."	9. Don't take yourself too seriously.
10. It's impossible to fail.	10. Drink lots of water, and keep breathing!

CLEARING PLAN—WEEKLY WORKSHEET

Week #_____ Dates _____

Every Day—Choose *at least one* practice from *each* of the four pathways.

1. **Intention:** To relieve stress, quiet the mind, and center myself, I will do my best to practice these Softening Attitudes [identify one or more phrases] _____ for _____ minutes, once a day, every day this week.

2. **Action:** I will [circle one] *sweep, put away, round up, clean, clear, or address* the following [identify one] *thing, pile, area, issue, toleration* _____ every day this week.

3. **Non-identification:** I will be mindful of these "shoulds" ____ _____; I will consciously reframe unpleasant and negative experiences with *"This is …"*; I will stop and feel as often as I remember and do my best to allow any weather to surface without taking it personally.

4. **Compassion:** I will do [this] _____ _____ to support myself, lighten up, and feel good; I will practice the Floor Pose every day this week.

Once This Week—Fill in as needed and check off when complete.

_____ 1. Address toleration(s):

_____ 2. Record feelings, shifts, synchronicities, dreams, *ah-has*

_____ 3. Plan for next week (fill out new worksheet)

_____ 4. Other—I will add the following extra clearing tasks or practice(s) this week:

_____

_____

_____

_____

Fill in the following chart with your selected task, and check it off as it is completed.

My Clearing Plan

Daily	Mon	Tues	Wed	Thurs	Fri	Sat	Sun
Intention							
Action							
Non-identification							
Compassion							
Water Intake (oz. or # of glasses)							

CLEARING CIRCLE—STEPS FOR CREATING AND MAINTAINING A CLEARING SUPPORT GROUP

A clearing circle is to a group experience what the clearing journal is to the solo traveler. The guidelines for how to create a clearing circle are divided as follows and described in detail below:

◊   Starting a Group

◊   Sample Ground Rules

◊   Sample First Meeting—Organizing the Circle

◊   Sample Follow-up Meetings

◊   Secrets to Success

To learn what a clearing circle is and how it can help support your clearing (exponentially), please refer to chapter 49, "Join with Others."

For six sample meeting agendas, go to appendix 3.

STARTING A GROUP

Think of one to six people with whom you can imagine spending six to twelve weeks cultivating a clear home and a spacious life. Choose only people who are good listeners and whom you trust implicitly. Stay away from any friends or close family members that may make you feel self-conscious or uncomfortable. One way to know is to ask yourself: Can I be completely myself with this person? Would it be okay to cry and laugh and share some of my most embarrassing moments with her/him? Think of this group as a sounding board, a witness, a mirror for you as you begin to release the clutter.

Choose a person to act as host or hostess, timekeeper, and facilitator for the meeting, and rotate this position if it seems appropriate. Set up a time to meet regularly: once a week, once every two weeks, or once a month for a period of six to twelve weeks. After that time, you can evaluate, recommit, and add more weeks if you wish. If meeting in person is not possible, you can talk on the phone or set up a weekly conference call or Skype. Because the circle depends on everyone making a commitment to participate, agree to meet for a set period of weeks and decide as a group if there should be a consequence for missing a meeting.

Depending on the size of the group, allow a minimum of ninety minutes to two hours for each gathering. Kick off with an introductory evening, during which participants can meet each other, share their intentions, review the ground rules, and receive the first assignment (see Sample First Meeting outlined below). The first assignment could be to buy this book and start reading it prior to the opening gathering.

In appendix 3, there are six sample agendas which are easy to adapt to a weekly or monthly gathering. If it seems like too much for people to read and complete all the tasks that are suggested for your meeting, dial it back.

SAMPLE GROUND RULES

Read this sample list out loud and make sure it resonates with your group. Feel free to make any modifications.

◊ **Listening:** This is a listening group, not a counseling or advice-giving session; we are not here to fix anything or anyone.

◊ **Witnessing:** We are here simply to share our stories of triumph and challenge and to offer support by witnessing and not personalizing any weather patterns that may arise.

◊ **Quiet:** To hold a space for each other, we will do our best to avoid interrupting and side comments.

◊ **Confidentiality:** Everything we say here shall remain confidential.

- ◊ **Speaking:** We will go once around the circle at the beginning of each meeting to give everyone a chance to check in briefly if they choose. We will do our best to speak from our own experience; we will use the first person singular "I" to describe how we feel. The person sharing will hold a talking stick or object to indicate that she has the floor. Placing the object back in the center of circle will indicate that she's finished, and someone else is free to speak.

- ◊ **Attendance:** To establish a container that feels safe for everybody, we will attend all meetings, except in extenuating circumstances. [*Note:* It would be good to clarify what those exceptions might be and if there should be any consequences for multiple absences.]

- ◊ **On Time:** Out of respect for everyone in the group, we will do our best to begin and end on time.

- ◊ **Silence:** If no one chooses to speak, we will sit in silence, being mindful of the time allotted for this part of the meeting.

- ◊ **Timekeeping:** We will use a watch or timer, if necessary, to keep the sharing and discussion moving.

SAMPLE FIRST MEETING—ORGANIZING THE CIRCLE

Sit in a circle; circles promote listening and healing. If you're the host or facilitator, open the circle with a welcome and, if you wish, an inspiring quotation. Read the list of sample ground rules above or your group's revised version. You can also read aloud the Ten Truths about the Journey and Ten Keys to Lasting Success summarized in "An Ongoing Journey" in this book.

Once you've established your ground rules and set the tone for your circle, begin with a once-around sharing session, using the three prompts below (or some variation) and a talking stick or object. Be mindful that this part of the sharing can bring up some weather.

1. Why I am here

2. What clutter represents for me; how it shows up in my life; how it makes me feel

3. What I hope might happen as a result of being in this group

Spend most of the first meeting exploring your hopes, fears, challenges, and intentions, and remember to honor the ground rules that you have just established.

After everybody has had a turn to share, discuss the logistics for your gatherings. Consider a reasonable timeframe, such as number of weeks, length of session, facilitator, and whether or not to rotate the venue.

Set a date, time, and place for your next meeting, and review the tasks for your next gathering from the first week's agenda (see appendix 3).

Close the circle with an appreciation, an insight, and/or an inspiring quotation to end on an "up" note. Alternatively, you can conclude with the Ten Truths and the Ten Keys, if you haven't read them already.

SAMPLE FOLLOW-UP MEETINGS

Begin with a welcome, an inspiring quotation, or an appreciation. Review the ground rules, if necessary. Consider opening the circle with a set of Softening Attitudes. These meditations are great ways to help quiet the mind and set a tone.

Follow with a quick check in. Go around the circle and invite each person to share anything that has surfaced during the previous week or month. Be mindful that side comments and interrupting can be a sign of nervous chatter (weather). If you are the host/facilitator for this gathering, bring people back gently if this happens and remind the group to speak only when they have the "talking stick."

After everyone has had a chance to speak once, you can either repeat the once-around or open up the circle to discuss the central themes and the questions outlined in the agenda.

Allow discussion time in the early weeks to review some of the Growing Pains and Signposts of Clutter Clearing presented in chapter 46. Ask if anyone is experiencing any clearing side effects, such as fatigue, moodiness, forgetfulness, mental fog, excessive energy, compulsive behaviors, and so on. You can also discuss the strategies that have worked well to mitigate discomfort, sluggishness, etc. (*Note:* This is an important aspect of the clearing journey; it brings up the opportunity to clear more weather.)

Conclude by going over your goals and tasks for the week (or month) ahead. Use a clearing plan worksheet (see appendix 1) to help focus and manage the task load, if it seems appropriate.

Decide on the next meeting date, time, and place.

Close the circle with each person sharing one word about how they are feeling in the moment. If you have a little extra time, consider closing a gathering with a simple meditation.

SECRETS TO SUCCESS

To receive the most from your clearing circle experience, I invite you to consider these three keys:

1. **Follow the ground rules.** Creating a sacred trust among all the members will insure the most important key to your success: safety. When we feel safe, we are more likely to let go.

2. **Allow silence.** Silence creates openings and opportunities to feel; don't be afraid of it!

3. **Allow mystery.** Consider this group experience as if you were journeying off road into the mystery of your own heart. There are no right or wrong answers. No one can predict or know what will happen. Whatever happens is all that can.

CLEARING CIRCLE— SIX SAMPLE MEETING AGENDAS

Because clutter (and talk of clutter) has a sneaky way of pressing buttons and throwing us off course, I have created six sample meeting agendas that you can use to help keep your gatherings energized and on point.

Note: For step-by-step guidelines on how to set up and maintain a successful clearing support group, see appendix 2.

MEETING #1—AWARENESS

Circle Discussion: Use this agenda after everyone in the group has read part 1. Complete the following, and add more as time and energy permit.

1. **Begin** [First meeting only]
   ◊ Share your name, why you're here, and how you hope to benefit from being in this group. [*See* Sample First Meeting— Organizing the Circle in appendix 2.]

2. **Describe**
   ◊ what "spaciousness" means to you, how it manifests in your life, and how it makes you *feel.*
   ◊ an experience you've had of letting go and what it felt like.

3. **Share**
   ◊ how your body gives you feedback; which of your six senses you tend to use the most.

◊ some of the ways you tap your intuition or source of inner guidance; how you know if the signals you're receiving are true and reliable.

◊ what it feels like to hang out in not knowing.

4. **Discuss themes**
   ◊ Use the summary highlights in part 1 to guide your discussion further (time permitting).

5. **Plan next meeting**
   ◊ logistics, time, and place

MEETING #2—INTENTION

Circle Discussion: Use this agenda after everyone in the group has read part 2. Complete the following, and add more as time and energy permit.

1. **List highs and lows**
   ◊ synchronicities, shifts, or *ah-has* you are experiencing

   ◊ any emotional "bumpy weather" that you are noticing as you work with this book

2. **Describe**
   ◊ what it feels like to say: "Everything I need is provided for."

   ◊ what it feels like to say: "Things work out for me without my having to try" (if different from how you feel about the above statement).

   ◊ what this means to you: "The universe is a neutral place that responds simply to my focus of attention."

3. **Share**
   ◊ how setting an intention makes a difference in your life (e.g., do you always get a place to park if you hold an intention for a spot to open up?).

   ◊ your personal list of ways to "act as if."

   ◊ what it feels like to express gratitude; any shifts and openings that you have noticed in your life as a result of expressing gratitude more often.

◊ your favorite letting-go rituals and what it feels like to do them.

◊ what it feels like after practicing Simple Meditation 1—Enough.

4. **Discuss themes**
   ◊ Use the summary highlights in part 2 to guide your discussion further (time permitting).

5. **Plan next meeting**
   ◊ logistics, time, and place

MEETING #3—ACTION

Circle Discussion: Use this agenda after everyone in the group has read part 3. Complete the following, and add more as time and energy permit.

1. **List highs and lows**
   ◊ synchronicities, shifts, or *ah-has* you are experiencing

   ◊ any weather patterns that you are noticing as you work with this book

2. **Describe**
   ◊ what it feels like to say: "I honor and value my things."

   ◊ what it feels like to say: "I honor and value myself" (if different from above).

   ◊ what it feels like to say: "It is safe for me to slow down and take my time."

3. **Share**
   ◊ what it feels like to put away the same thing, round up the same area, or sweep every day.

   ◊ clearing tasks that bring up resistance; thoughts that might feed your resistance.

   ◊ the effects, if any, that have rippled out as a result of adopting the R&R (reduce and repeat) method of clearing (both physical clutter and behaviors you'd like to change).

   ◊ what it feels like after practicing Simple Meditation 2—Ease.

○ your list of tolerations (housekeeping tasks, issues, or projects that need fixing, finishing, or tending to) and what it was like to address one of them.

4. Discuss themes

○ Use the summary highlights in part 3 to guide your discussion further (time permitting).

5. Plan next meeting

○ logistics, time, and place

MEETING #4—NON-IDENTIFICATION

Circle Discussion: Use this agenda after everyone in the group has read part 4. Complete the following, and add more as time and energy permit.

1. List highs and lows

○ synchronicities, shifts, or *ah-has* you are experiencing

○ any weather patterns that you are noticing as you work with this book

2. Describe

○ what it feels like to say, "I am not my story. I am not my drama."

○ what it feels like to say, "I am bigger than my clutter" (if different).

3. Share

○ what it means to "unplug" and how you know that you have succeeded.

○ instances where you have successfully detached from an outcome and what it felt like.

○ what it feels like to "lean in" to physical pain or a difficult emotional situation and whether taking this counterintuitive step eased the discomfort.

○ what it feels like after practicing Simple Meditation 3—Allow.

4. Discuss themes

○ Use the summary highlights in part 4 to guide your discussion further (time permitting).

5. **Plan next meeting**
   ◊ logistics, time, place

MEETING #5—COMPASSION

Circle Discussion: Use this agenda after everyone in the group has read part 5. Complete the following, and add more as time and energy permit.

1. **List highs and lows**
   ◊ synchronicities, shifts, or *ah-has* you are experiencing
   ◊ any weather patterns that you are noticing as you work with this book

2. **Describe**
   ◊ what it feels like to say, "I deeply and completely accept myself."
   ◊ what it feels like to say, "Pleasure is my birthright" (if different).

3. **Share**
   ◊ what you did this week to nourish and care for yourself; how easy or difficult it was.
   ◊ reasons you might resist caring for yourself.
   ◊ what it feels like to do the Floor Pose every day.
   ◊ what it was like to take yourself out on a solo date; what you chose to do and why.
   ◊ your list of ways that open you to experiencing pure joy.
   ◊ a list of things that make you laugh (e.g., funniest movies, books, jokes).
   ◊ what it feels like after practicing Simple Meditation 4—Rest.

4. **Discuss themes**
   ◊ Use the summary highlights in part 5 to guide your discussion further (time permitting).

5. **Plan next meeting**
   ◊ logistics, time, and place

MEETING #6—WISDOM

Circle Discussion: Use this agenda after everyone in the group has read part 6. Complete the following, and add more as time and energy permit.

1. **List highs and lows**
   - ◊ synchronicities, shifts, or *ah-has* you are experiencing
   - ◊ any weather patterns that you are noticing as you work with this book

2. **Describe**
   - ◊ what it feels like to say: "It is safe for me to reveal my true self."
   - ◊ what it feels like to say: "I trust that I'll know what to do next."

3. **Share**
   - ◊ ways that clearing has proven to be more than what you thought it might be.
   - ◊ the effects, if any, that have rippled out as a result of adopting a "slow drip" approach to clearing every day.
   - ◊ ways that you will be prepared the next time you see someone in your life that caused you pain.
   - ◊ how you know that "you cannot grow yourself by yourself" and steps that you'll take to seek support in the weeks ahead.

4. **Discuss themes**
   - ◊ Use the summary highlights in part 6 to guide your discussion further (time permitting).

5. **Plan next meeting**
   - ◊ logistics, time, and place

FOR FURTHER INSPIRATION

BOOKS AND ARTICLES

Beattie, Melody. *The Language of Letting Go Journal: A Meditation Book and Journal for Daily Reflection.* Center City, MN: Hazelden, 2003.

Cameron, Julia. *The Artist's Way: A Spiritual Path to Higher Creativity.* New York: Jeremy P. Tarcher/Putnam, 1992.

Chödrön, Pema. *When Things Fall Apart: Heart Advice for Difficult Times.* Boston, MA: Shambhala Publications, 2002.

———. *The Places That Scare You: A Guide to Fearlessness in Difficult Times.* Chapter 22, "The In-Between State." Boston, MA: Shambhala Publications, 2005.

———. *Taking the Leap: Freeing Ourselves from Old Habits and Fears.* Boston, MA: Shambhala Publications, 2009.

Emoto, Masaru. *The Hidden Messages in Water.* Translated by David A. Thayne. Hillsboro, OR: Beyond Words Publishing, 2004.

Heider, John. *The Tao of Leadership: Lao Tzu's Tao Te Ching Adapted for a New Age.* Atlanta, GA: Humanics New Age, 1985.

Hicks, Esther, and Jerry Hicks. *Ask and It Is Given: Learning to Manifest Your Desires.* Carlsbad, CA: Hay House, 2004.

Johnson, Robert A. *Owning Your Own Shadow: Understanding the Dark Side of the Psyche.* San Francisco: HarperSanFrancisco, 1991.

Katie, Byron. *Loving What Is: Four Questions That Can Change Your Life.* New York: Harmony Books, 2002.

———. *Who Would You Be without Your Story?* Carlsbad, CA: Hay House, 2008.

Maurer, Robert. *One Small Step Can Change Your Life: The Kaizen Way.* New York: Workman, 2004.

McTaggart, Lynne. *The Field: The Quest for the Secret Force of the Universe.* New York: HarperCollins, 2002.

Naparstek, Belleruth. *Your Sixth Sense: Activating Your Psychic Potential.* San Francisco: HarperSanFrancisco, 1997.

Nhat Hanh, Thich. *Present Moment, Wonderful Moment: Mindfulness Verses for Daily Living.* Berkeley, CA: Parallax Press, 1990.

Norris, Gunilla. *Being Home: A Book of Meditations.* Photographs by Greta D. Sibley. New York: Bell Tower, 1991.

Pert, Candace. *Molecules of Emotion: Why You Feel the Way You Feel.* New York: Scribner, 1997.

Pollan, Michael. *In Defense of Food: An Eater's Manifesto.* New York: Penguin Press, 2008.

Richardson, Cheryl. *The Art of Extreme Self-Care: Transform Your Life One Month at a Time.* Carlsbad, CA: Hay House, 2009.

Rilke, Rainer Maria. *Letters to a Young Poet.* Translated by M. D. Herter Norton. New York: W.W. Norton & Company, 1954.

Tolle, Eckhart. *The Power of Now: A Guide to Spiritual Enlightenment.* Novato, CA: New World Library, 1999.

Vienne, Vèronique. *The Art of Doing Nothing: Simple Ways to Make Time for Yourself.* Photographs by Erica Lennard. New York: C. Potter, 1998.

Ware, Bronnie, *The Top Five Regrets of the Dying: A Life Transformed by the Dearly Departing.* Carlsbad, CA: Hay House, 2012.

Yogananda, Paramahansa. *Autobiography of a Yogi.* New York: Philosophical Library, 1946.

WEB ESSAYS AND BLOG POSTS

"The Art of Doing Nothing," by Leo Babauta, http://zenhabits.net/the-art-of-doing-nothing/.

"The First Thing You Do When You Sit at the Computer," by Seth Godin. *Seth Godin's Blog,* http://sethgodin.typepad.com/, January 12, 2012.

Steve Jobs's Stanford University Commencement Address. June 12, 2005. Text and video, http://news.stanford.edu/news/2005/june15/jobs-061505.html/.

"Enough," by Merlin Mann, in *What Matters Now,* compiled by Seth Godin, December 2009. Free eBook at http://sethgodin.typepad.com/seths_blog/2009/12/what-matters-now-get-the-free-ebook.html/.

"Home," by Stephanie Bennett Vogt, http://www.lifebyme.com/stephanie-bennett-vogt-home/.

Stephanie Bennett Vogt's essays on simplifying, reinvention, and letting go in the *Huffington Post,* http://www.huffingtonpost.com/stephanie-bennett-vogt/.

"National Day of Unplugging: Can You Spend 24 Hours Offline?" by Margaret Wheeler. *Huffington Post,* http://www.huffingtonpost.com/2012/03/23/national-day-of-unplugging_n_1371220.html, March 23, 2012.

ONLINE RESOURCES

Clear Your Home, Clear Your Life; twenty-eight-day online course; www.dailyom.com

Emotional Freedom Techniques; www.thetappingsolution.com

Fly Lady; a clutter-clearing website; www.flylady.net

Freecycle Network; recycle your old stuff; www.freecycle.org

Meetup; organize an online group; www.meetup.com

National Association of Professional Organizers; www.napo.net

Oprah Winfrey's Lifeclass; Oprah Winfrey Network (OWN); www.oprah.com

Reclaim Your Mailbox; www.41pounds.org

Skype; www.skype.com

Stephanie Bennett Vogt; www.spaceclear.com

Super Soul Sunday; Oprah Winfrey Network (OWN); www.oprah.com

Svaroopa Yoga; www.svaroopayoga.org

Your Spacious Self; thirty-day free email series; www.spaceclear.com/resources/free-email-series

Zen Habits; www.zenhabits.net

AUDIOS, VIDEOS, AND MOVIES

Chödrön, Pema. *Getting Unstuck.* Audiobook. Louisville, CO: Sounds True, 2006.

Dorfman, Andrea, and Tanya Davis. *How to Be Alone.* Video. http://youtube/k7X7sZzSXYs/.

The Ellen Show. "Ellen's Favorite Moments: Meeting Gladys." Video. http://ellen.warnerbros.com/gladys_hardy/.

MacDonald, Kevin (director). *Touching the Void.* Movie starring Joe Simpson and Simon Yates, 2004. Two men's thrilling and disastrous climb of the remote and treacherous Siula Grande in Peru. An incredible account of tragedy, friendship, and human endurance.

The Shadow Effect: Illuminating the Hidden Power of Your True Self. Docudrama featuring bestselling authors Debbie Ford, Deepak Chopra, Marianne Williamson, et al. June 26, 2009. http://theshadoweffect.com/.

Shadyac, Tom (director). *I AM.* Documentary featuring some of today's notable thinkers in science, philosophy, academia, and spirituality. 2010. http://www.iamthedoc.com/thefilm/.

ABOUT THE AUTHOR

Stephanie Bennett Vogt, MA, is New England's leading space clearing expert and a contributing author of *Pearls of Wisdom,* with Jack Canfield, Marci Shimoff, et al., and *The Thought That Changed My Life Forever.* She brings more than thirty-five years of experience to SpaceClear, the teaching and consulting practice that she founded in 1996 to help homes and their occupants come into balance. Stephanie teaches her inspirational clearing programs at centers worldwide, including Kripalu and the New England School of Feng Shui, and shares her unique perspectives on simplifying, personal reinvention, and letting go as a course contributor at *DailyOM* and a columnist for the *Huffington Post.* Stephanie and her husband divide their time between Concord, Massachusetts, and San Miguel de Allende, Mexico. Please see her website at www.spaceclear.com.

Hierophant Publishing
8301 Broadway, Suite 219
San Antonio, TX 78209
888-800-4240

www.hierophantpublishing.com